Engineering Economics - The Basics

Second Edition

For Kori

"Engineering economics is a mad science, don't expect to get the monster correct every time."

Website: www.NieKo.com

ABOUT

I am a full time bridge engineer and owner of the blog, tallbridgeguy.com. I currently teach engineering economics at the local university and in the past I have taught Structural Analysis, Reinforced Concrete Design, Introduction to Hydrology / Hydraulics, 3D modeling, REVIT and Construction Management. A number of video examples are located on my YouTube channel, youtube.com/user/acceleratedbridge.

I am not an economist; I am a working engineer that uses economics on a daily basis.

LAYOUT OF THE BOOK

This second edition is intended as a supplemental text for engineering students taking an undergraduate course in engineering economics. Videos and additional information for this book will also be posted on NieKo.com.

Although every effect has been made to ensure the accuracy of each example, readers should always check the given results. I would appreciate feedback on any errors in the book and I will correct them as soon as possible.

Mistakes in spelling and grammar should be expected (Hey I'm an engineer!) but I will try to fix them as soon as possible.

FAMOUS ENGINEERS YOU SHOULD KNOW!

I have added some links to Wikipedia© pages, featuring Engineers, every aspiring or current engineer should know. I can't vouch for the veracity of the wiki pages but they often have good images!

CONTENTS

CHAPTER 1 - INTRODUCTION TO ENGINEERING ECONOMICS

1) INTRODUCTION

WHY DO ENGINEERS NEED TO LEARN ECONOMICS?

OVERVIEW

Well the first obvious reason, because you want to graduate.

To be honest, engineering economics is not the most exciting course of study for engineers. Typically, most engineering degree programs require just one course in economics to satisfy graduation requirements. But, as a practicing bridge engineer, I can tell you that the ability to use money wisely is a skill sorely needed in the field.

For example, I have to constantly evaluate what type of structure would be the best fit for a given site. Should it be a concrete bridge, a steel bridge or a bridge made with new composite materials? The field of Accelerated Bridge Construction (ABC) is also becoming big business in the bridge world and engineers have to evaluate the cost of building a bridge in a weekend vs. the conventional practice of building the bridge over a few months.

ECONOMIC ANALYSIS

Economic decisions break down into three main areas, simple, intermediate, and political. Simple decisions really do not take economics into account, for example, buying a cup of coffee. A benefit cost ratio is not going to change your mind if you need a hit of caffeine. (And who would take the time to do it. Well an engineer might..)

Intermediate decisions are the sweet spot for engineering economics. The information needed for the analysis can generally be quantified and using formulas, with rational assumptions, a "best" alternative can be chosen. Should you build a $5 million dollar bridge that will last 50 years or a $7 million bridge that will last 75 years? How does the costs associated with maintenance of the bridge, over its life, add to the decision?

Political economics are outside the realm of this book, because all the economic analysis in the world is no match for a power broker picking the final alternative. This happens a great deal in the engineering world. For example, you can have the greatest economic analysis ever made and the client could just say naaa, I want that one. So be careful getting your hopes up for a rational decision if political implications are lurking in the background.

INTERMEDIATE ECONOMIC ANALYSIS

Okay this is where we are going to focus our energies. Your client or boss has asked for your help in picking the best alternative for a project and you are going to use economic factors as the basis for that decision. Usually this means the winner is the alternative that costs the least or the one that makes the most money.

The one huge caveat to picking the best alternative is the old programming adage, "garbage in, garbage out." This means your chosen alternative may not actually be the best one but it may be the best one based on your chosen economic criteria. Choosing the "correct" appropriate criteria is the only way to get a meaningful result.

Economic analysis is not always straight forward with easy to find accurate numbers for every variable, work hour or future maintenance cost. Decisions have to be made on a "best assumption" basis. For example, bridges typically need a new deck overlay, (the top two inches of the riding surface) every 20 years on average. If you used this assumption in an analysis but you really needed a new deck overlay for the bridge in 15 years it could affect which project was actually the most desirable.

Be honest about the assumptions you make and be aware of the limitations of the chosen criteria. Small errors can lead to large problems when you are dealing with money and the long life spans of engineering projects.

2) INCOME, BENEFITS AND COSTS

In teaching engineering economics we always seem to leave out the reason for all our cool calculations. We are trying to forecast how much we owe over time on our mortgage, which alternative is the right one and how long do I have to save for that beautiful restored green Gremlin. (It's a car!)

Essentially, we are bringing financial factors into our decision making process using the time value of money. Time value of money is a fancy way of saying we have to consider the interest rate on the money used for the project under consideration. Most individuals and business pay interest on money they borrow or receive interest on money they invest. A good alternative can turn into a poor one if the interest rate changes. Also determining the most accurate interest rate for our calculations can be difficult if the life span of the project is long. For example, how much faith can we have in assessing an interest rate 20 years from now? Still an accurate interest rate is the first step in our calculations.

Next we have to consider benefits and costs. Take for example a small store owner. She will have benefits in the form of payments from consumers for her products, but she will have costs, like buying inventory, rent, power, shipping, etc. Her income is equal to her benefits minus her costs. Now this is considered gross income and her net income would be her gross income minus taxes, retirement plan contributions, etc.

In this book we will not deal with the effects of taxes, deductions and retirement plans. We are going to keep it simple and compare alternatives on the basis of benefit and costs, using a set interest rate.

3) INTEREST FORMULAS AND NOMENCLATURE

The following interest formulas are the basis for the examples given throughout this book. Couple the formulas with a good cash flow diagram and you can do a lot of economic damage but in a good way.

TABLE 1 – INTEREST FORMULAS

		Interest Tables
SIMPLE COMPOUND INTEREST FORMULAS		
To find F – Given P	$F = P(1+i)^n$	F = P(F/P,i,n)
To find P – Given F	$P = F(1+i)^{-n}$	P = F(P/F,i,n)
SERIES COMPOUND FORMULAS		
To find F – Given A	$F = A\left[\frac{(1+i)^n - 1}{i}\right]$	F = A(F/A,i,n)
SINKING FUND		
To find A – Given F	$A = F\left[\frac{i}{(1+i)^n - 1}\right]$	A = F(A/F,i,n)
CAPITAL RECOVERY		
To find A – Given P	$A = P\left[\frac{i(1+i)^n}{(1+i)^n - 1}\right]$	A = P(A/P,i,n)
SERIES PRESENT WORTH		
To find P – Given A	$P = A\left[\frac{(1+i)^n - 1}{i(1+i)^n}\right]$	P = A(P/A,i,n)
ARITHMETIC GRADIENT UNIFORM SERIES		
To find A – Given G	$A = G\left[\frac{(1+i)^n - in - 1}{i(1+i)^n - i}\right]$	A = G(A/G,i,n)
ARITHMETIC GRADIENT PRESENT WORTH		
To find P – Given G	$P = G\left[\frac{(1+i)^n - in - 1}{i^2(1+i)^n}\right]$	P = G(P/G,i,n)
GEOMETRIC GRADIENT		
Geometric Series Present Worth		
To find P – Given A_1, g When i=g	$P = A_1 n(1+i)^{-1}$	
To find P – Given A_1, g When i≠g	$P = A_1\left[\frac{1-(1+g)^n(1+i)^{-n}}{i-g}\right]$	

P = present sum of money	*A = end of period cash receipt or disbursement*
F = future sum of money	*G = uniform increase or decrease in a uniform series*
I = interest rate per interest period	*g = uniform rate of cash flow increase or decrease*
n = number of interest periods	*r = nominal interest rate per interest period*

CHAPTER 2 – DIFFERENT TYPES OF INTEREST

1) SIMPLE INTEREST

Simple interest is probably something you would only get from a relative. (Meaning, financial institutions stay away from it.) For example, you borrow $1000 dollars from your Uncle and he gives you a simple interest rate of 10% per year, for two years. on the loan. So at the end of two years you would owe him $1000 + $1000*0.10*2 = $1200.

Simple interest does not take into account any effects of compounding and stays the same every period. It is defined as Future worth (F) equal to the principle amount (P) times the interest rate per period (i) times the number of periods (n),

$$F = P + P*i*n \quad \text{or} \quad F = P+Pin$$

F – Future worth
P – Principle amount
i – Simple interest rate per period (typically per year)
n – Number of interest periods

Famous Engineers you should know!

Isambard Kingdom Brunel

(April 9, 1806 – September 15, 1859)

Brunel was an English engineer who designed dockyards, the Great Western Railway, and a series of innovative steamships. He also designed a number of groundbreaking bridges and tunnels, including the first tunnel under a navigable river and the Clifton Suspension Bridge spanning the Avon Gorge. Often ranked as one of the ten best engineers who ever lived. (Well at least by the British.)

EXAMPLE 2-1

So your parents forced you to take engineering instead of going to Art school like you planned. They did give you a $5000 dollar loan, with simple interest of 8% per year, to start the fall semester. How much do you have to pay back after 2 years, 5 years or ten years?

year

2 $F = P + Pin = \$5000 + 5000(.08)2$

$= \$5800.00$

5 $F = \$5000 + 5000(.08)5$

$= \$7000.00$

10 $F = \$5000 + 5000(0.08)10$

$= \$9000.00$

EXAMPLE 2-2

Emma borrows $2500 to buy a cement mixer so she can mix mortar for building concrete block walls. If she paid back $3750, what is the simple interest rate if she pays back the money at the end of a) 2 years?, b) 5 years?.

$$F = P + P \times i \times n$$

<u>2 years</u>

$$\$3750 = \$2500 + \$2500 \times i \times 2$$

$$i = 0.25 \Rightarrow \underline{\underline{25\%}}$$

<u>5 years</u>

$$\$3750 = \$2500 + \$2500 \times i \times 5$$

$$i = 0.1 \Rightarrow \underline{\underline{10\%}}$$

"One test is worth a dozen expert opinions"

EXAMPLE 2-3

How much would you have to invest now to have \$168,000 in 15 years at 9% simple annual interest rate?

$$F = P + Pin$$

$$\$168{,}000 = P + P(0.09 \times 15)$$

$$\$168{,}000 = P(1 + 0.09 \times 15)$$

$$P = \frac{\$168{,}000}{(1 + 0.09 \times 15)} = \underline{\underline{\$71{,}489.36}}$$

"It has always been important that people understand clearly the nature, the types of problems and the processes used by engineers. They use any fact or theory of science, wherever and however developed, that contributes to their art.

If a knowledge of physics, of chemistry, of meteorology, of mathematics is useful in attaining the ends in view, engineers will go to endless trouble to master these sciences for their purpose." Hardy Cross

EXAMPLE 2-4

A $5500 loan was to be repaid with 6% simple annual interest. A total of $6375 was paid. How long had the loan been outstanding?

$$F = P + Pin$$

$$6375 = 5500 + 5500(0{,}06)n$$

Solve for $n = 2{,}576$ years

$= 30{,}9$ months

"The most important thing is to keep the most important thing the most important thing."

— Donald P Coduto

2) NOMINAL AND COMPOUNDING INTEREST

Nominal interest is the interest rate for a given period without considering the effects of compounding. Typically, a year is used for the time period and a lowercase r, is used to denote the interest rate.

r – Nominal interest rate per time period (typically a year)

For example, credit card statements will show a nominal interest rate for your credit card. This is not the interest rate you pay for the use of their money. (This is not the interest rate you are looking for...if you get this you really are an engineer) Your monthly credit card payments are based on the effective interest rate.

Compounding interest is often described as paying interest on top of interest. In the chart below you can see how it works. At the beginning of year one you have a present worth (sum of money). After one year you have present worth plus the interest rate X present worth which equals = P + i*P or P(1+i). Essentially, your beginning of period sum earns additionally money in the form of interest at the end of every period. This is compounding interest.

Year	Amount at beginning of interest period	+ interest for period	= Amount at end of interest period
1	P	$+ iP$	$= P(1+i)$
2	$P(1+i)$	$+ iP(1+i)$	$= P(1+i)^2$
3	$P(1+i)^2$	$+ iP(1+i)^2$	$= P(1+i)^3$
4	$P(1+i)^3$	$+ iP(1+i)^3$	$= P(1+i)^4$
5	$P(1+i)^4$	$+ iP(1+i)^4$	$= P(1+i)^5$
n	$P(1+i)^{n-1}$	$+ iP(1+i)^{n-1}$	$= P(1+i)^n$

Notice how this develops the compound amount formula, **$F=P(1+i)^n$** (bottom far right column), described in the next chapter. An example may help to sort this out.

EXAMPLE 2-5

If you deposit $100 dollars in a mutual fund that earns a 10% interest rate, compounded yearly, how much will you have in the fund in five years?

year	Beginning of year	+ end of year	= Total
1	$100	+ 0.10(100)	= $110
2	$110	+ 0.10(110)	= $121
3	$121	+ 0.10(121)	= $133.10
4	$133.10	+ 0.10(133.10)	= $146.41
5	$146.41	+ 0.10(146.41)	= $161.05

$$F = P(1+i)^n = 100(1+0.10)^5$$

$$= 161.05$$

"Engineering problems are under-defined, there are many solutions, good, bad and indifferent. The art is to arrive at a good solution. This is a creative activity, involving imagination, intuition and deliberate choice."

— Ove Arup

3) EFFECTIVE INTEREST

Effective interest is the annual interest rate taking into account any compounding during the year. Credit cards often quote a yearly nominal interest rate and then compound the interest monthly so the effective rate per year is different (higher) than the nominal rate. This makes them more money, go figure.

r – Nominal interest rate per time period (typically a year)
i – Effective interest rate for a given period
i_a – Effective interest rate per year
m – Number of compounding sub periods per time period

$$i_a = (1+r/m)^m - 1$$ (effective interest rate per year)

or

$$i_a = (1+ RP)^m - 1$$

where

RP – interest rate per period

EXAMPLE 2-6

You decided to start a concrete driveway business for the summer and used your credit card to buy $3000 dollars worth of lumber for forming the concrete. If your credit card has a nominal rate of 15%, what is your effective interest rate per month and per year?

Rate per month

$$\frac{15\%}{12 \text{ months}} = \frac{1\frac{1}{4}\%}{\text{month}}$$

$$i_a = \left(1 - \frac{r}{m}\right)^m - 1 = \left(1 - \frac{0.15}{12}\right)^{12} - 1$$

$$= (1 + 0.0125)^{12} - 1$$

$$= 0.161 = \underline{\underline{16.1\%}}$$

So you are really paying an effective interest rate of 16.1% per year because the interest is compounded monthly and not yearly. Tricky, huh.

EXAMPLE 2-7

The yearly effective interest rate of a nominal 9% interest rate, compounded quarterly is

$i_a = (1+r/m)^m - 1 = (1 + 0.09/4)^4 - 1 = 0.09308 = \underline{\underline{9.31\%}}$

EXAMPLE 2-8

A debt of $20,000 must be paid in a series of equal monthly payments for 5 years. The nominal annual interest rate is 10%, compounded monthly. What is the effective interest rate for this loan?

$i_a = (1+r/m)^m - 1 = (1 + 0.10/12)^{12} - 1 = 0.1047 = \underline{\underline{10.5\%}}$

EXAMPLE 2-9

What is the future worth of \$1000 in one year, at 10% nominal interest rate, compounded quarterly?

Interest rate per quarter $= \frac{0.10}{4} = \underline{.025}$

$$F = P(1+i)^n = 1000(1+.025)^4$$

$$= \$1103.81$$

Compounding quarters	\$ + i		
1	1000 + 1000(.025)	=	1025
2	1025 + 1025(.025)	=	1050.63
3	1050.63 + 1050.63(.025)	=	1076.89
4	1076.89 + 1076.89(.025)	=	1103.81

$$i_a = \left(1 + \frac{.10}{4}\right)^4 - 1 = .1038 = 10.38\% \text{ effective}$$

Using effective interest rate

$$F = 1000(1+.1038)^1 = \$1103.81$$

EXAMPLE 2-10

You have borrowed \$2000 from the bank and have to make 12 equal payments of \$180.60 to pay the loan back.
Determine
1) the effective monthly interest rate
2) the nominal annual interest rate
3) the effective annual interest rate.

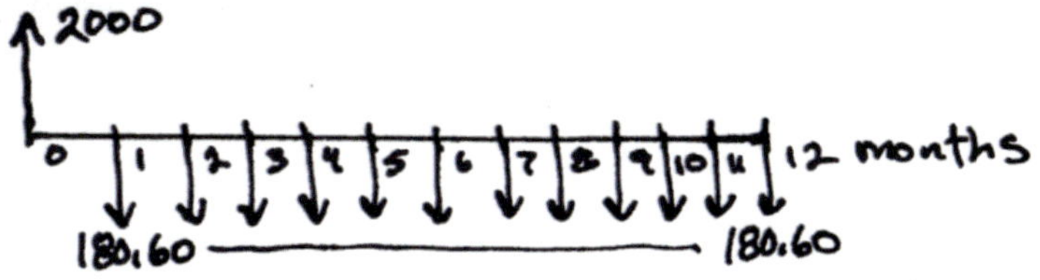

$$P = A\left[\frac{(1+i)^n - 1}{i(1+i)^n}\right] \Rightarrow 2000 = 180.60\left[\frac{(1+i)^{12} - 1}{i(1+i)^{12}}\right]$$

$$\frac{2000}{180.60} = 11.074 = \left[\frac{(1+i)^{12} - 1}{i(1+i)^{12}}\right]$$

Calculator Solver

① $i = .01257/\text{month}$

② $.01257/\text{month} \times 12 \text{ months} = .15084 = 15.084\%$

③ $i_a = \left(1+\frac{r}{m}\right)^n - 1 = \left(1+\frac{.15084}{12}\right)^{12} - 1 = .1617 = 16.17\%$

or

$i_a = (1+.01257)^{12} - 1 = .1617 = 16.17\%$

CHAPTER 3 – CASH FLOW DIAGRAMS

1) YES YOU DO NEED TO DRAW A CASH FLOW DIAGRAM!

If you are just starting out in engineering economics, drawing a cash flow diagram (CFD) is one of the best ways to fully understand a problem. Cash flow diagrams represent all the money coming in and going out of an economic endeavor. By drawing a CFD you can often see clearly the unknown you are trying to find with your analysis.

A) OVERVIEW AND GUIDELINES

Guidelines for drawing cash flow diagrams are,

1) Positive cash flows are drawn going up and negative cash flows are drawn going downwards.
2) Typically, cash flows are shown at the end of the time period. (end of month, end of year, etc)
3) Cash flows should be drawn to scale.
4) Do not combine cash flows on a CFD so individual cash flows are easier to read.
5) Cash flows diagrams depend on the point of view. A seller will have a different CFD than a buyer.
6) Be careful comparing alternatives with different life spans. Often a common denominator life span will be used between alternatives with the assumption that cash flows remain the same but are just repeated.

Examples of cash flows values:

Benefits – positive cash flows
Costs – negative cash flows
Salvage value – end of life cash flow (estimated, because you really never know the true future value)
Operation and maintenance – costs to keep your machinery or operation running (ie mortgages)
Repairs or overhaul – cost to fix your equipment

Typical Cash flow Diagram

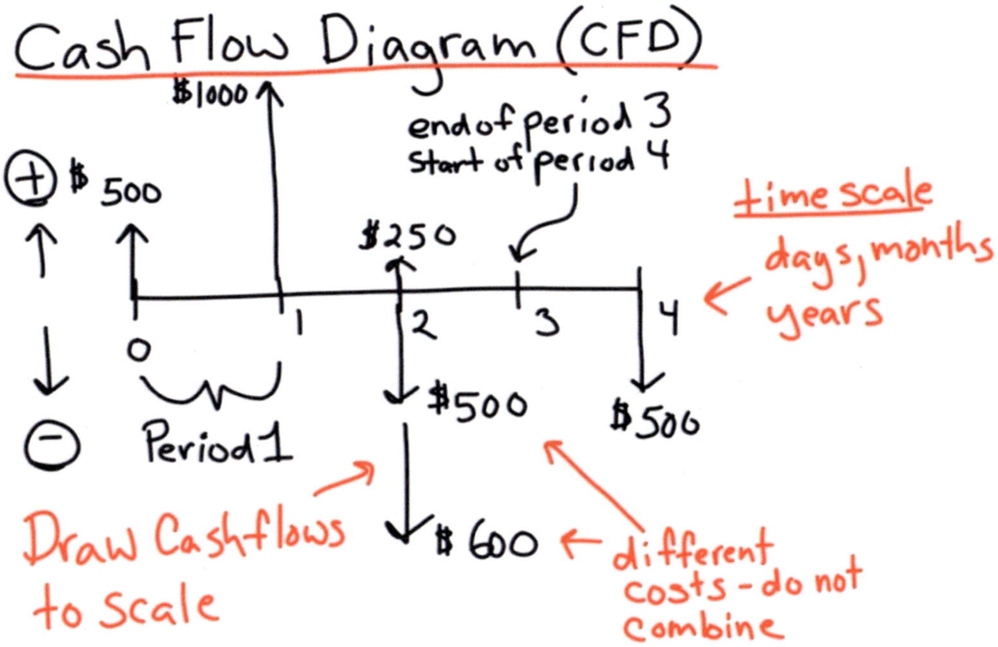

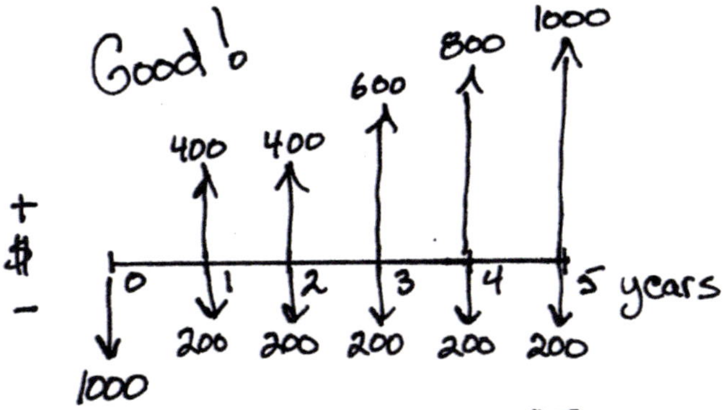

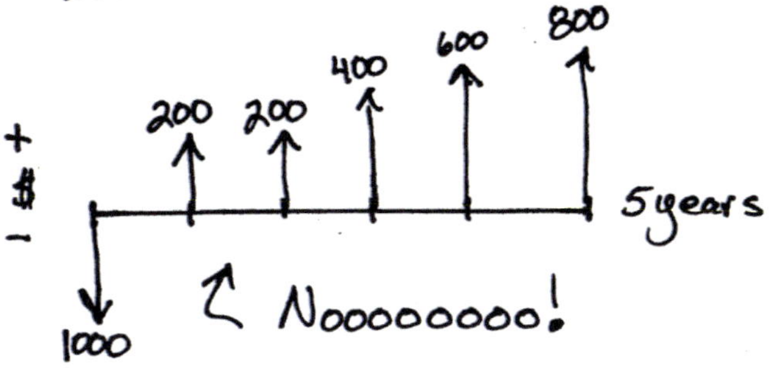

EXAMPLE 3-1

You want to start a crane rental business, so you decide to buy a 2013 Grove RT880E – 80 Ton Rough Terrain Crane. The seller asks for a down payment of $80,000 and then $40,000 a year for 10 years. You are assuming about $8,000 a year for operation and maintenance (O&M) (gas, oil, etc) with a salvage value (SV) of $50,000 at the end of ten years. Profit per year is estimated to be $70,000 and you anticipate having to replace the tires in the fifth year for a price of $4,000.

Draw the cash flow diagram.

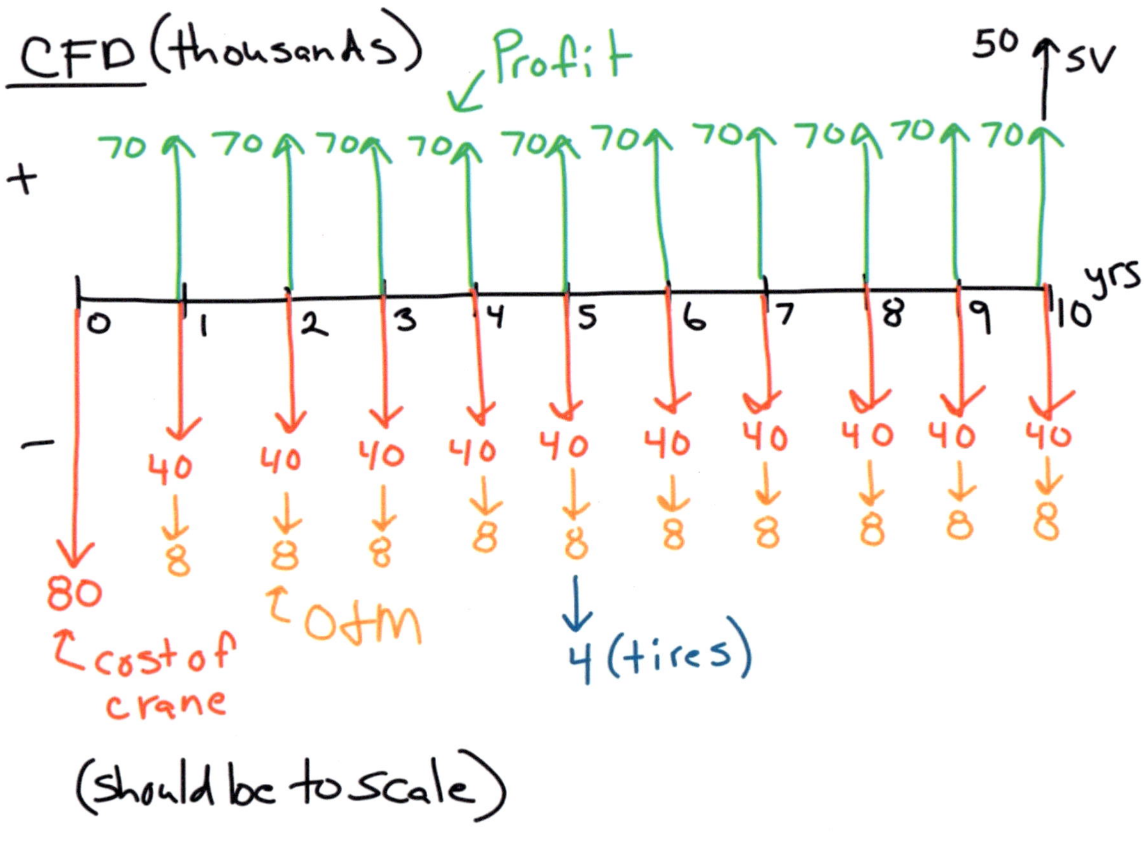

Example 3 -1 in excel, showing the net present value (NPV) calculation using an interest rate of 5%.

year	First cost	payments	O&M	tires	Profit	salvage	total
0	-80000						-80000
1		-40000	-8000		70000		22000
2		-40000	-8000		70000		22000
3		-40000	-8000		70000		22000
4		-40000	-8000		70000		22000
5		-40000	-8000	-4000	70000		18000
6		-40000	-8000		70000		22000
7		-40000	-8000		70000		22000
8		-40000	-8000		70000		22000
9		-40000	-8000		70000		22000
10		-40000	-8000		70000	50000	72000
					present	worth=	**$117,439.73**

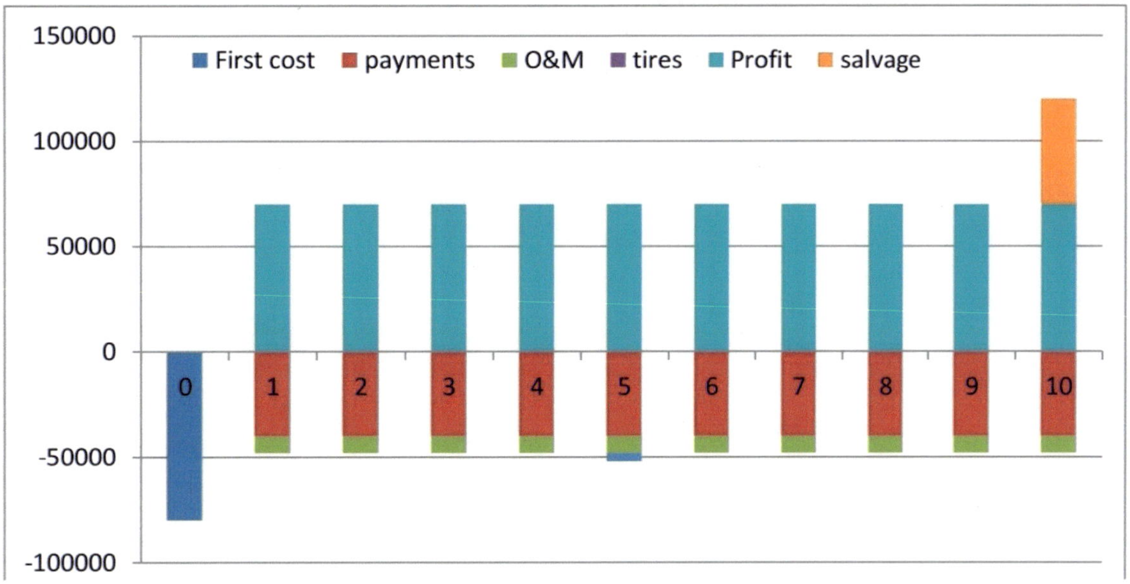

The excel formula for the net present worth of the Total column is =-8000+NPV(rate, value 1, value 2, etc)

EXAMPLE 3-2

Your engineering firm was awarded a total sum of $50,000 to design a new bridge for the City of Hope. You will be paid $10,000 immediately and $5,000 at the end of the 1st, 2nd, 3rd,4th and 5th months. You will receive the remaining balance after obtaining approval for the city council at the end of the 6th month.

1) Draw the cash flow diagram for your firm.
2) Draw the cash flow diagram for the City of Hope.
3) Draw the cash flow diagram, for your firm, if you have to hire a structural engineer to help with this job for four months at $4,000 per month.

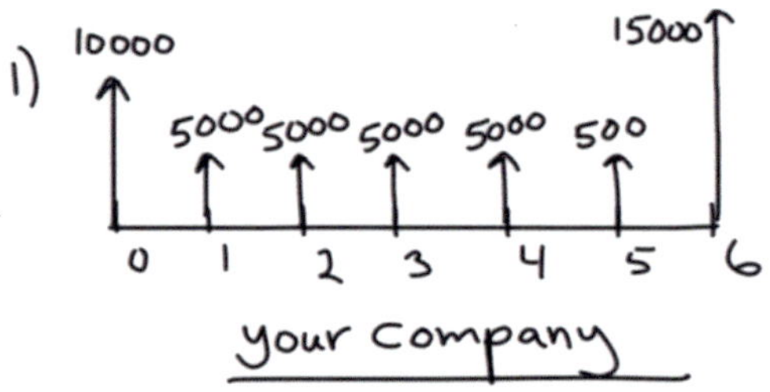

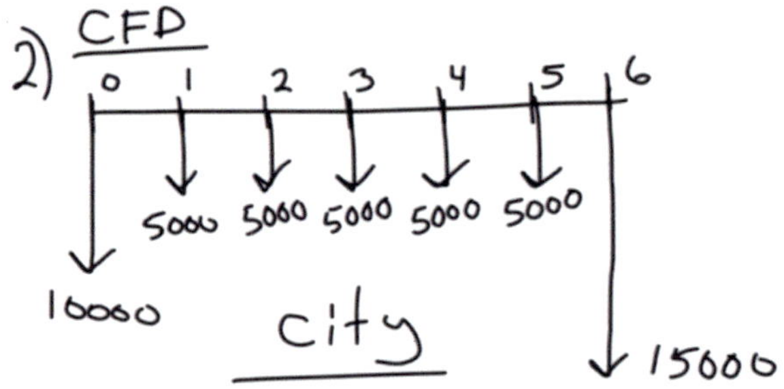

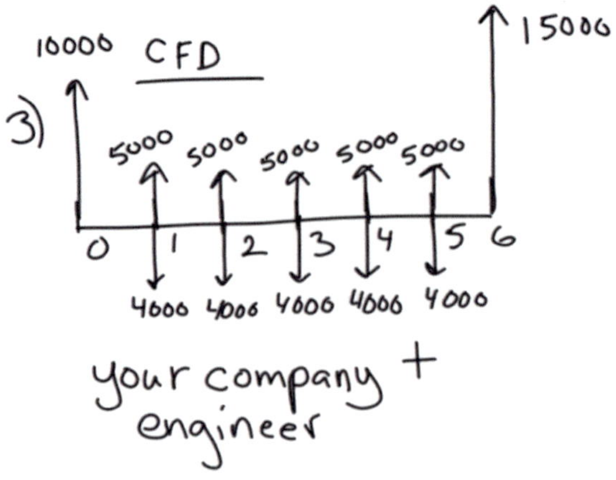

EXAMPLE 3-3

A contractor bough a 20 ton mobile crane for $100,000. The monthly expense of fuel was $2,000 and the company gernerated a monthly income of $5,000 by renting out the crane. At the end of the 6th month, a hose on the crane leaked and required $6,000 in repairs. At the end of the 12th month, the contractor decided to sell the crane for $75,000. Draw the cash flow diagram for the crane.

Note: I was a little lazy on the CFD below. I should have labeled the time units and what each payment was for…

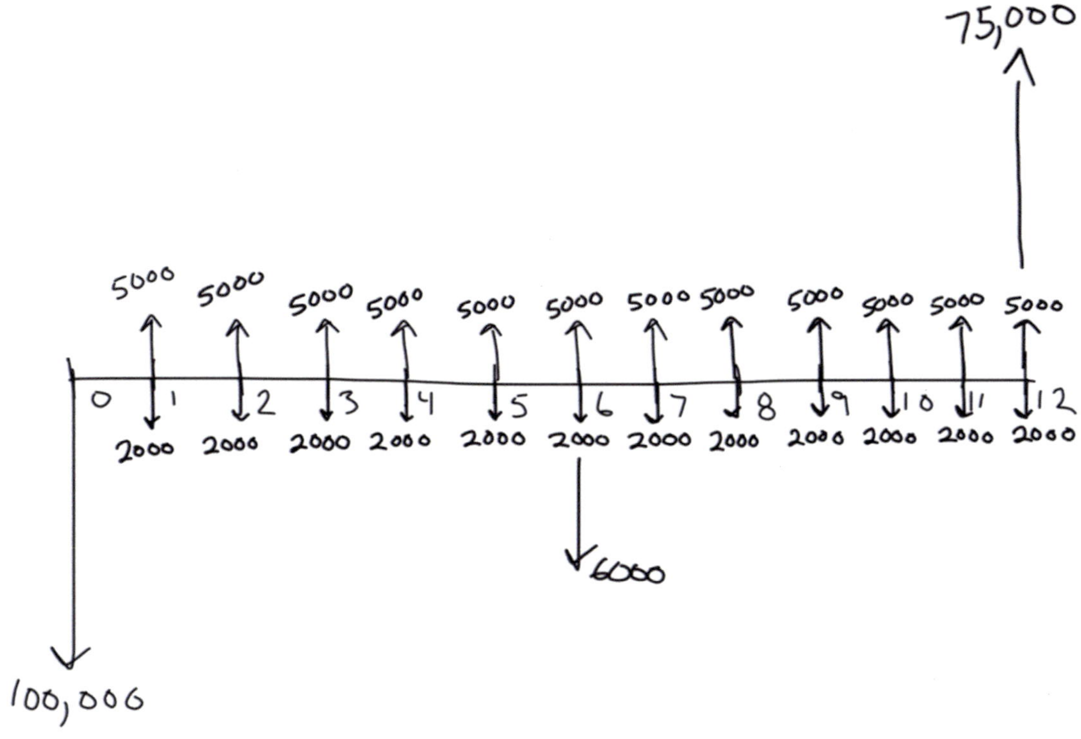

CHAPTER 4 – SIMPLE COMPOUNDING FORMULAS

1) COMPOUND AMOUNT (SINGLE FUTURE WORTH)

The compound amount formula finds the future worth of a present value using the compounding effect of interest. It is good for "what if" scenarios, such as, if I deposited money now how much will it be in the future.

$$F = P(1 + i)^n$$

F – Future worth
P – Present Worth
i – Interest rate per period
n – Number of interest periods

Famous Engineers you should know!

Conde Balcom McCullough

(May 30, 1887 – May 5, 1946)

Conde McCullough graduated from Iowa State College in 1910.

In 1919 he became the head of the Bridge Division of the Oregon Department of Transportation, making him personally responsible for the design of Oregon's bridges at a time when the state was completing Highway 101.

He helped design over 600 bridges, many with architectural details such as Gothic spires, art deco obelisks, and Romanesque arches incorporated into the bridges.

McCullough is considered by many as being one of the top ten bridge engineers of all time and advocated that "bridges be built economically, efficiently, and with beauty."

p.s. he is my favorite bridge engineer!

EXAMPLE 4-1

You deposit a $1000 dollars in a mutual fund account that pays 5% interest per year. How much money will you have in the account at the end of ten years? The compound amount formula finds the future worth of a present value using the compounding effect of interest.

Present worth (P) = $1000   Interest rate (i) = 5% = 5/100 = 0.05   Number of time periods (n) = 10

$$F = P(1+i)^n$$

$$F = \$1000\left(1+\frac{5}{100}\right)^{10}$$

$$F = \$1628.89$$

4-1

$$F = P(1+i)^n = 1000(1.6289) = \$1628.89$$

← from interest tables

EXAMPLE 4-2

You want to determine if your engineering degree will be worth the effort. Assuming a starting salary of $47,000, that grows at a rate of 4% per year, how much money will you be making in a) 5 years? B) 10 years? C) 40 years?

a) 5 years

$$F = P(1+i)^n = 47{,}000(1+0.04)^5 = \$57{,}182.69$$

b) 10 years

$$F = P(1+i)^n = 47{,}000(1+0.04)^{10} = \$69{,}571.48$$

c) 40 years

$$F = P(1+i)^n = 47{,}000(1+0.04)^{40} = \$225{,}647.97$$

4-2

a) $F = P(1+i)^n = 47{,}000(1.2167) = \$57{,}182.69$

b) $F = P(1+i)^n = 47{,}000(1.4802) = \$69{,}569.40$

c) $F = P(1+i)^n = 47{,}000(4.8010) = \$225{,}647$

from interest tables

EXAMPLE 4-3

If you currently have $3750 in the bank, growing at 3.5% nominal interest per year, and you need $7500 dollars to buy your dream surveying transit, how many months do you have to wait before you can buy the transit? Assume the bank compounds your savings account interest monthly. (Using natural log or just use your calculator and guess!)

$$i/\text{month} = \frac{0.035}{12} = 0.00292/\text{month} \leftarrow \text{Interest rate per month}$$

$$F = P(1+i)^n \quad \underline{n = ?}$$

$$7500 = 3750(1+0.00292)^n$$

$$\frac{7500}{3750} = (1.00292)^n \Rightarrow 2 = (1.00292)^n$$

$$\ln 2 = \ln(1.00292)n$$

$$n = \frac{\ln 2}{\ln(1.00292)} = 237.7 = \underline{\underline{238 \text{ months}}}$$

(about 19.8 years!)

EXAMPLE 4-4

How much money would Mary have in five years if she was paid $2000 today, $2500 a year from now and $5000 three years from now if the interest rate remained at 9% per year?

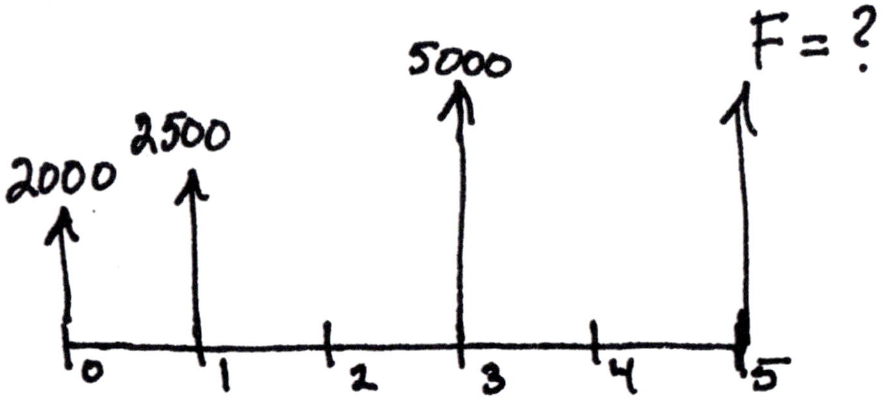

$$F = P(1+i)^n$$

$$F = 2000(1+0.09)^5 + 2500(1+0.09)^4 + 5000(1+0.09)^2$$

$$= \$12,546.70$$

EXAMPLE 4-5

You want to buy a pan vibrator for your concrete pouring business. If you deposit \$2000 in the bank for three years and you get \$3250 back, what was the interest rate the bank gave you?

- assume monthly compounding

$n = 3 \times 12 \text{ months} = 36$

$$F = P(1+i)^n$$

$$3250 = 2000(1+i)^{36}$$

$$\frac{3250}{2000} = 1.625 = (1+i)^{36}$$

$$(1.625)^{1/36} = (1+i)$$

$$1.01357 = 1+i$$

$$i = .01357 = \underline{1.357\%}$$

per month

2) PRESENT WORTH – (SINGLE PRESENT WORTH)

The present worth formula finds the present worth of a future sum based on compounding interest. This is the flip side to the previous compound amount formula. You can use it to plan for future events, for example, I need $40,000 to go college in five years, how much do I have to deposit in the bank today to get there?

$$P = F(1 + i)^{-n}$$

P – Present Worth
F – Future worth
i – Interest rate per period
n – Number of interest periods

Famous Engineers you should know!

Santiago Calatrava

(July 28, 1951 – present)

Calatrava is a Spanish architect, sculptor and structural engineer currently living in New York City.

From Wikipedia

"Calatrava has defined his style as bridging the division between structural engineering and architecture. In his projects, he claims to continue a tradition of Spanish modernist engineering that included Félix Candela, Antonio Gaudí, and Rafael Guastavino, with a very personal style that derives from numerous studies of the human body and the natural world. Architecture critics, however, see his work as a continuation of the expressionism of Eero Saarinen."

Probably the most famous bridge designer living today.

EXAMPLE 4-5

If you wanted $10,000 in the bank five years from now, how much money would you have to deposit today, if your bank paid 7% interest compounded yearly?

$$P = F(1+i)^{-n}$$
$$P = 10{,}000(1+0.07)^{-5} = \underline{\$7129.86}$$

EXAMPLE 4-6

You want to retire after a long satisfying career in engineering with $1,575,250 dollars in the bank. If you work for 40 years, how much money would you have to put in the bank now, earning 5% nominal interest per year, to reach that goal?

a) Assuming the bank compounds interest yearly,

b) if the bank compounded monthly?

$$P = F(1+i)^{-n}$$
$$\text{a) } P = 1{,}575{,}250(1+0.05)^{-40} = \underline{\underline{\$223{,}757.46}}$$
$$\text{b) } \frac{i_a}{\text{month}} = \frac{0.05}{12} = 0.00417/\text{month}$$
$$P = 1{,}575{,}250(1+0.00417)^{-(40\times12)} = \underline{\underline{\$214{,}074.57}}$$

Using Interest Table

4-6

$$\text{a) } P = F(1+i)^{-n} = 1{,}575{,}250(0.1420) = \underline{\$223{,}685.50}$$

Note: The difference between using the formula and the interest table are due to the number of significant figures. Interest table numbers are rounded to four decimal places.

EXAMPLE 4-7

What is the present worth of payments if Mary was paid $2000 today, $2500 a year from now and $5000 three years from now if the interest rate remained at 9% per year?

Year	Paid
0	$2000
1	$2500
2	
3	$5000

$$P = F(1+i)^{-n}$$

$$P_0 = 2000 + 2500(1+0.09)^{-1} + 5000(1+0.09)^{-3} = \$8154.49$$

Extra

$$F_{5\text{ years from now}} = P(1+i)^n = 8154.49(1+0.09)^5$$

$$F_5 = \$12,546.70$$

EXAMPLE 4-8

What is the present sum equivalent to $9525 two years from now, if interest is 6% per 6-month period?

$$P = F(1+i)^{-n}$$

2 years = 4 x 6 month periods

$$P = 9525(1+0.06)^{-4} = \$7544.69$$

CHAPTER 5 – UNIFORM SERIES COMPOUNDING FORMULAS

1) COMPOUND AMOUNT – UNIFORM SERIES

This formula is used to find a single future worth based on a series of uniform cash flows. You can use it to plan for retirement, for example, if you deposit $500 per month for twenty years, how much will you have at the end of twenty years?

$$F = A\left[\frac{(1+i)^n - 1}{i}\right]$$

F – Future worth
A – Uniform series cash benefit or cash cost amount
i – Interest rate per period
n – Number of interest periods

Famous Engineers you should know!

Thomas Telford

(1757–1834)

Telford was a Scottish civil engineer, architect and stonemason who designed roads, bridges and canals.

From Wikipedia

"Such was his reputation as a prolific designer of highways and related bridges, he was dubbed The Colossus of Roads, and, reflecting his command of all types of civil engineering in the early 19th century, he was elected as the first President of the Institution of Civil Engineers, a post he retained for 14 years until his death."

EXAMPLE 5-1

If you paid $2500 a year for your crane payment, for 10 years, at 5% interest, how much did you pay at the end of 10 years? Assume the salvage value is $5,000.

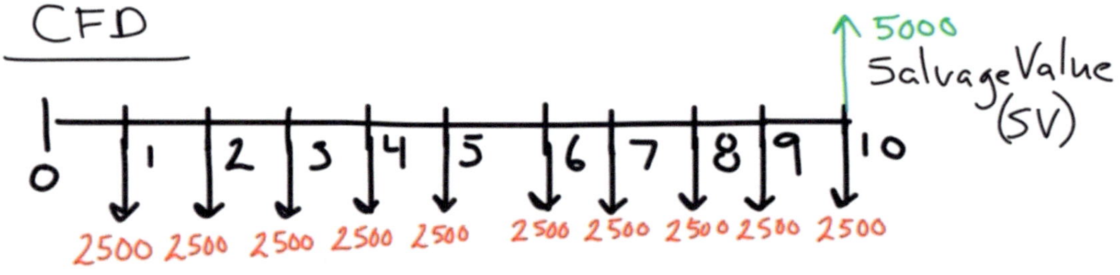

Want 2

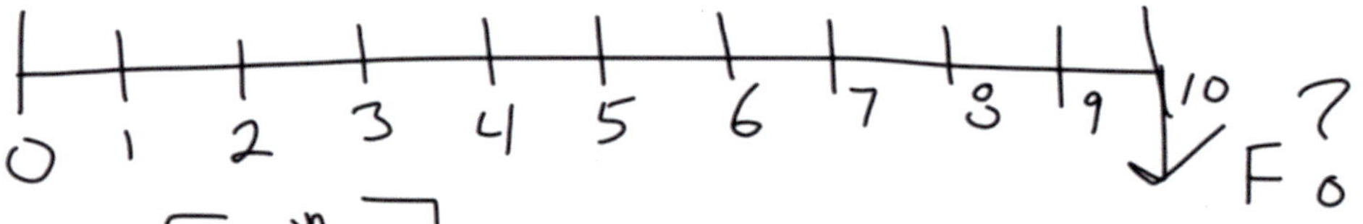

$$F = A\left[\frac{(1+i)^n - 1}{i}\right] + SV$$

neg

$$F = {}^{-}2500\left[\frac{(1+0.05)^{10} - 1}{0.05}\right] + 5000 = {}^{-}26{,}444.73$$

5-1) Using Interest tables

$$F = A\left(F/A, i, n\right) + SV$$

$$F = {}^{-}2500\left(F/A, 5\%, 10\right) + 5000$$

$$F = {}^{-}2500\left(12.5779\right) + 5000 = {}^{-}\$26{,}444.73$$

EXAMPLE 5-2

Find the future value, in year six, of the cash flow shown below using an annual interest rate of 8%.

Solution: You have four equal benefits of \$200 and you want to know the future value of the money in year six. You can do this a number of different ways, here is one way of doing it.

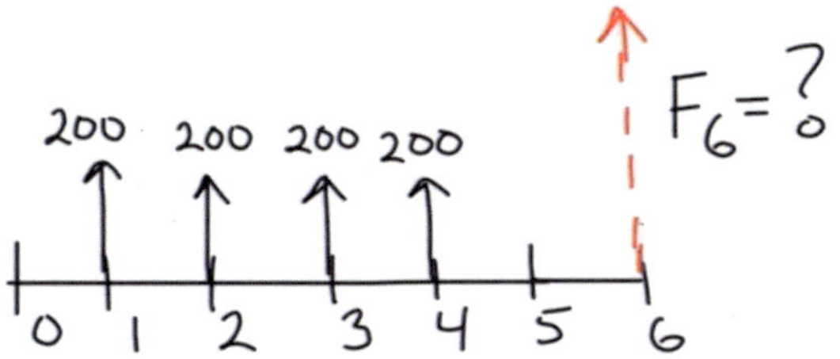

① move A (\$200) to year 4

$$F_4 = A\left[\frac{(1+i)^n - 1}{i}\right] = 200\left[\frac{(1+0.08)^4 - 1}{0.08}\right] = \underline{901.22}$$

② move F_4 to F_6

$$F_6 = P(1+i)^n = F_4(1+i)^n = 901.22(1+0.08)^2 = \underline{\underline{\$1051.19}}$$

"The engineer's first problem in any design situation is to discover what the problem really is."

— Unknown

2) SINKING FUND – UNIFORM SERIES

The sinking fund formula is used to determine a uniform series of cash flows that will culminate in a future worth. For example, imagine you want $50,000 in the bank 10 years from now, how much (A) would you have to deposit every month to get there?

$$A = F\left[\frac{i}{(1+i)^n - 1}\right]$$

A – Uniform series cash benefit or cash cost amount
F – Future worth
i – Interest rate per period
n – Number of interest periods

Famous Engineers you should know!

Robert Maillart

(February 6, 1872 – April 5, 1940)

A Swiss engineer, Mailart revolutionized the use of structural reinforced concrete.

From Wikipedia

His completed Salginatobel (1929–1930) and Schwandbach (1933) bridges changed the aesthetics and engineering of bridge construction dramatically and influenced decades of architects and engineers after him. In 1991 the Salginatobel Bridge was declared an International Historic Civil Engineering Landmark by the American Society of Civil Engineers.

EXAMPLE 5-3

If you want to have one million dollars in the bank in 20 years, (to buy that concrete truck you always wanted) how much would you have to save every month at a nominal interest rate of 11%?

NOTE: The problem is using monthly time periods and not years, so you have to determine a monthly interest rate.

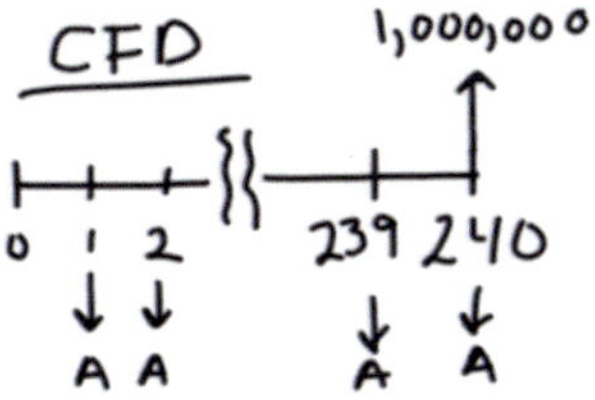

months

$20 \text{ years} \times 12 = \underline{240}$

$i/\text{month} = 11\%/12 = .917\% \Rightarrow 0.00917/\text{month}$

$$A = F\left[\frac{i}{(1+i)^n - 1}\right] = 1{,}000{,}000\left[\frac{0.00917}{(1+0.00917)^{240} - 1}\right] = \$1155.22/\text{month}$$

note you are saving for $n = 240$ months

"I guess the question I'm asked the most often is: "When you were sitting in that capsule listening to the count-down, how did you feel?" Well, the answer to that one is easy. I felt exactly how you would feel if you were getting ready to launch and knew you were sitting on top of two million parts -- all built by the lowest bidder on a government contract."

— John Glenn

3) CAPITAL RECOVERY – UNIFORM SERIES

This is probably one of the most useful interest formulas. The capital recovery formula determines a uniform series of cashflows that would equal a present worth. The obvious example is a car payment. If the car cost $10,000 today, how much would I have to pay every month for five years to pay back the $10,000 (plus interest)?

$$A = P\left[\frac{i(1+i)^n}{(1+i)^n - 1}\right]$$

A – Uniform series cash benefit or cash cost amount
P – Present Worth
i – Interest rate per period
n – Number of interest periods

Famous Engineers you should know!

John Roebling

(June 12, 1806 – July 22, 1869)

Roebling is best known for his wire rope suspension bridge designs and the design of the Brooklyn Bridge.

From Wikipedia

"In 1867 Roebling started design work on what is now called the Brooklyn Bridge, spanning the East River in New York. One day in 1869 he was standing at the edge of a dock, working on fixing the location where the bridge would be built, when his foot was crushed by an arriving ferry."

EXAMPLE 5-4

You just bought a concrete saw for $4500 with a five year loan period. How much do you have to pay per month, for those five years if the nominal interest rate is 8% per year?

CFD

5 years = 60 months

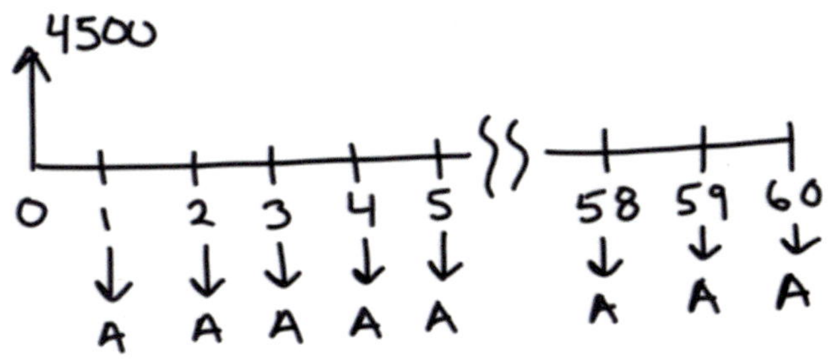

$$\frac{8\%}{12} = 0.667\%/\text{month} = 0.00667$$

$$A = P\left[\frac{i(1+i)^n}{(1+i)^n - 1}\right] = 4500\left[\frac{0.00667(1+0.00667)^{60}}{(1+0.00667)^{60} - 1}\right]$$

$$A = \$90.76/\text{month for 60 months}$$

"I am, and ever will be, a white-socks, pocket-protector, nerdy engineer, born under the second law of thermodynamics, steeped in steam tables, in love with free-body diagrams, transformed by Laplace and propelled by compressible flow."

— Neil Armstrong

EXAMPLE 5-5

A loan of $2000 is to be repaid in four equal semiannual (every 6 months) payments. If the annual interest rate is 5% compounded semiannually, how much is each payment?

$$A = P\left[\frac{i(1+i)^n}{(1+i)^n - 1}\right] \qquad \frac{5\%}{2\text{ periods}} = 2.5\%/6\text{months}$$

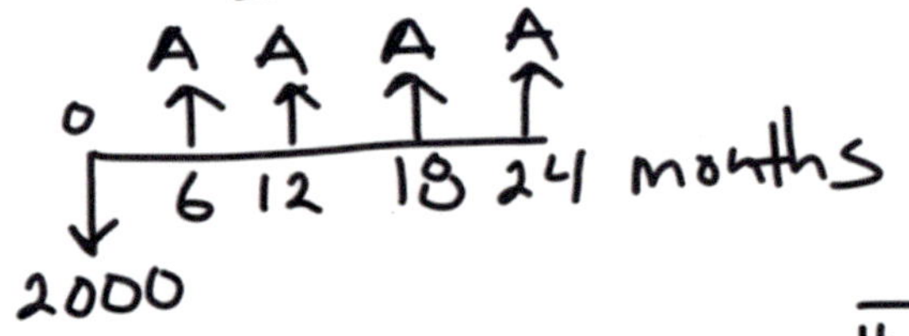

$A = ?$

$$A = 2000\left[\frac{0.025(1+0.025)^4}{(1+0.025)^4 - 1}\right] = \$531.64$$

5-5) Using Interest tables

* do not have a 2.5% table so interpolate.

$i = 2\%$, $n = 4$ periods

$$(A/P, 2\%, 4) = .2626$$

$i = 3\%$, $n = 4$ periods

$$(A/P, 3\%, 4) = .2690$$

$$\frac{(.2626 + .2690)}{2} = .2658 \approx (A/P, 2.5\%, 4)$$

$$A = 2000(A/P, 2.5\%, 4)$$

$$A = 2006(.2658) = \$531.60$$

4) PRESENT WORTH – UNIFORM SERIES

This formula calculates the present worth of a series of uniform cashflows. It is very useful for comparing alternative economic plans (which we will get to).

$$P = A\left[\frac{(1+i)^n - 1}{i(1+i)^n}\right]$$

P – Present Worth
A – Uniform series benefit or cost amount
i – Interest rate per period
n – Number of interest periods

Famous Engineers you should know!

Joseph Strauss and Charles Alton Ellis

Joseph Baermann Strauss (January 9, 1870 – May 16, 1938) was an American structural engineer, best known for being the chief engineer of the Golden Gate Bridge.

Charles Alton Ellis (1876–1949) was a professor, structural engineer and mathematician who was chiefly responsible for the structural design of the Golden Gate Bridge. Because of a dispute with Joseph Strauss, he was not recognized for his work when the bridge opened in 1937.

EXAMPLE 5-6

You want to buy a forklift to help you move short precast concrete beams around your plant. You can afford to pay $575 per month, if you take a six year loan at 7% interest, how much can you pay for a forklift today?

CFD

$n = 6 \times 12 = 72$ months

Assume 7% per year

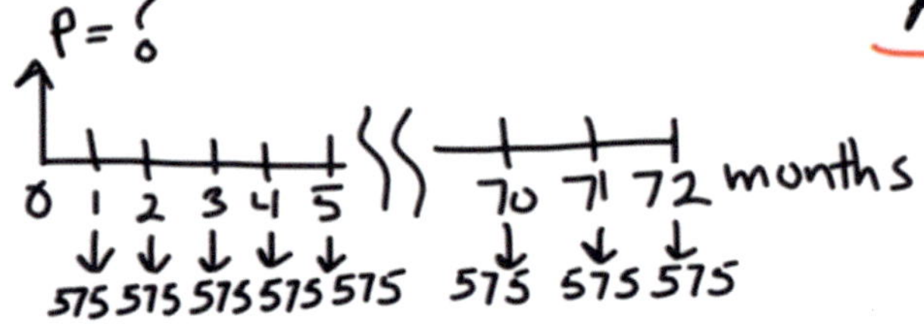

$$\frac{7\%}{12\text{ months}} = \frac{0.583\%}{\text{month}} = 0.00583$$

$$P = A\left[\frac{(1+i)^n - 1}{i(1+i)^n}\right]$$

$$P = 575\left[\frac{(1+0.00583)^{72} - 1}{0.00583\,(1+0.00583)^{72}}\right] = \$33{,}730.11$$

EXAMPLE 5-7

You want to start a crane rental business, so you decide to buy a 2013 Grove RT880E – 80 Ton Rough Terrain Crane. The seller asks for a down payment of $80,000 and then $40,000 a year for 10 years. You are assuming about $8,000 a year for operation and maintenance (O&M) (gas, oil, etc) with a salvage value of $50,000 at the end of ten years. Profit per year is estimated to be $70,000 and you anticipate having to replace the tires in the fifth year for a price of $4,000.

Is this a profitable economic model, if the nominal interest rate is 5%? Use a present worth analysis to decide. Draw the Cash Flow Diagram

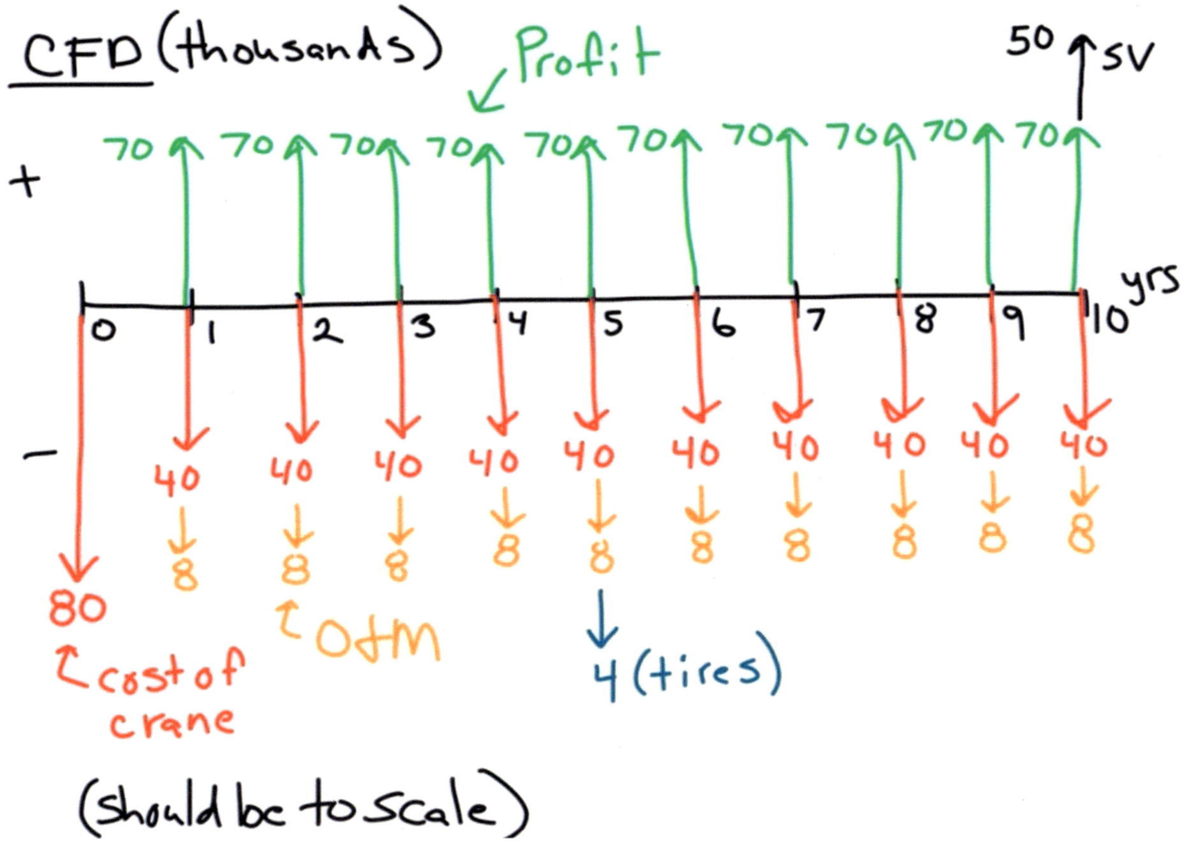

Example 5-7 cont. Perform the Calculations

Present Worth Analysis

$$P = A\left[\frac{(1+i)^n - 1}{i(1+i)^n}\right] + F(1+i)^{-n}$$ ← using series & single payment

neg ↘

$$P = -\$80{,}000 + (70{,}000 - 48{,}000)\left[\frac{(1+0.05)^{10} - 1}{0.05(1+0.05)^{10}}\right]$$

$$\overset{SV}{+\,50{,}000}(1+0.05)^{-10} - 4000(1+0.05)^{-5}$$

$$= +\$117{,}439.73$$

Positive present worth = good alternative

CHAPTER 6 – GRADIENT COMPOUNDING FORMULAS

An arithmetic gradient is a constant value (sum of money) change between multiple time periods. Take a look at the figure below and take note where the gradient actually starts. This often leads to a lot of calculation errors, if you miss this point.

Assuming an increasing series,

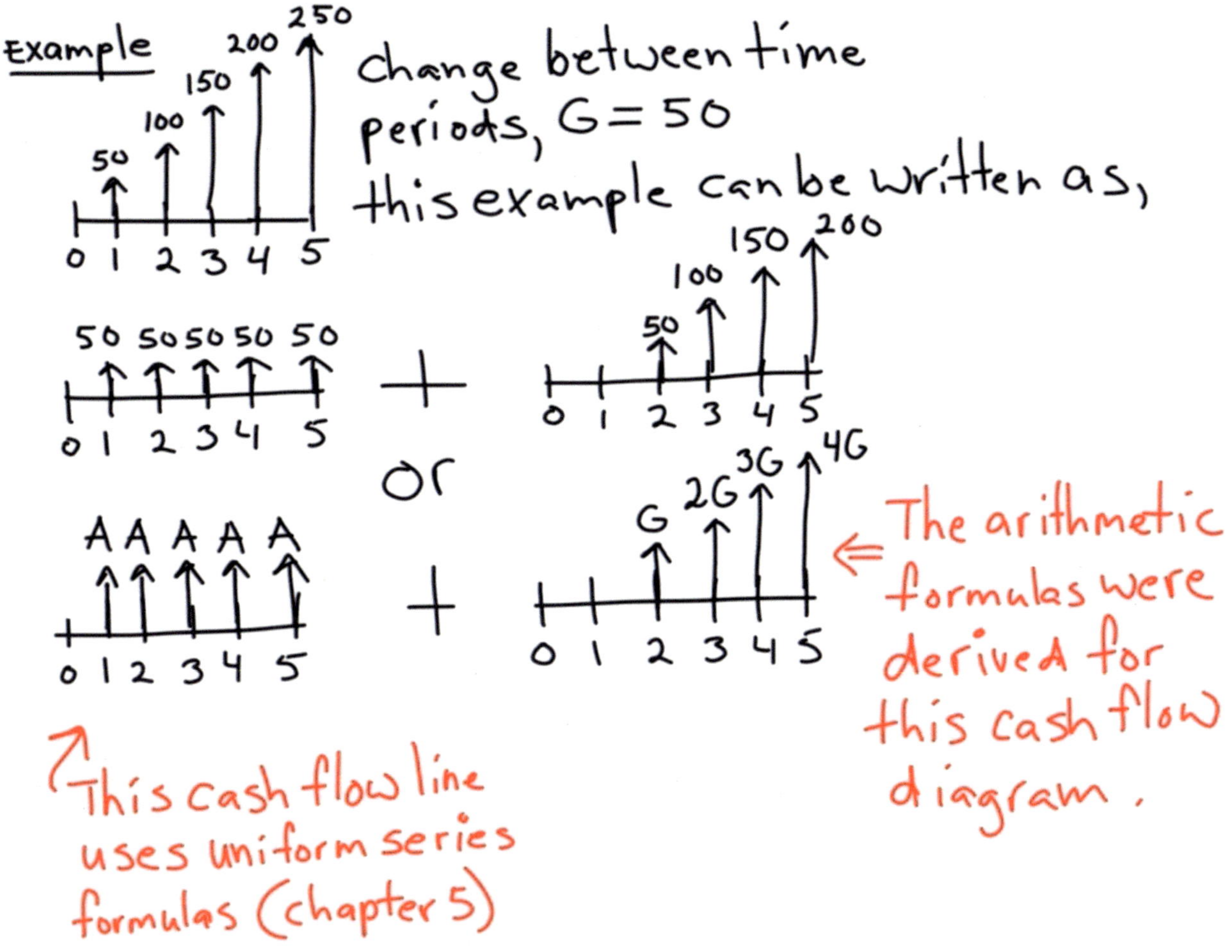

1) ARITHMETIC GRADIENT - UNIFORM SERIES

This formula determines a uniform series of cash flows based on a series of uniform gradient cash flows.

$$A = G\left[\frac{(1+i)^n - in - 1}{i(1+i)^n - i}\right]$$

A – Uniform series cash benefit or cash cost amount
G – uniform gradient benefit or cost amount
i – Interest rate per period
n – Number of interest periods

Famous Engineers you should know!

Gustave Eiffel

(December 15, 1832 – December 27, 1923)

Best known for something other than a bridge. (If you can't guess you are in trouble.) But he also designed some great bridges.

For example, the Maria Pia bridge and the Garabit viaduct.

EXAMPLE 6-1

Calculate the uniform annual benefit equivalent to the following cash flow if the annual interest rate is 8%. NOTE: the gradient starts in year two!

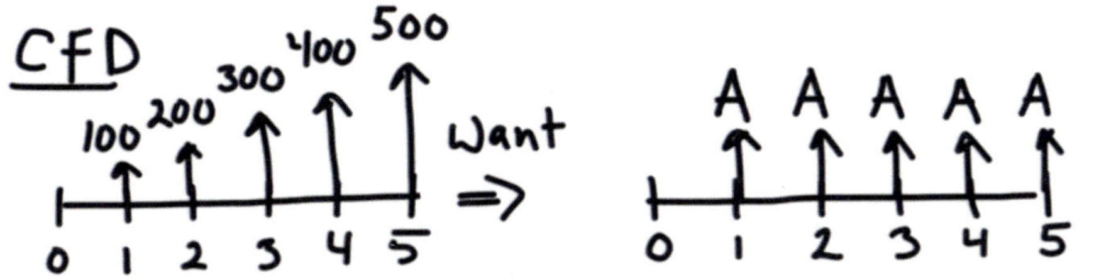

$$A = A + G\left[\frac{(1+i)^n - in - 1}{i(1+i)^n - i}\right]$$

$$A = 100 + 100\left[\frac{(1+0.08)^5 - 0.08(5) - 1}{0.08(1+0.08)^5 - 0.08}\right] = \$284.65$$

Note how the original cash flow can be separated into two equivalent cash flows. The second cash flow uses the arithmetic gradient uniform series formula.

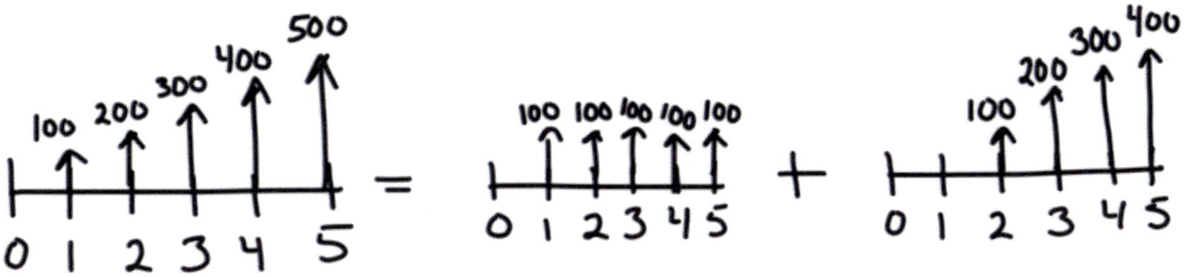

2) ARITHMETIC PRESENT WORTH – UNIFORM SERIES

This formula finds a Present Value based on a uniform gradient cash flow.

$$P = G\left[\frac{(1+i)^n - in - 1}{i^2(1+i)^n}\right]$$

P – Present Worth
G – uniform gradient benefit or cost amount
i – Interest rate per period
n – Number of interest periods

Famous Engineers you should know!

Christian Menn

(March 3, 1927 – present)

One of the great structural engineers with a great sense of style.

Take a look at the Sunniberg Bridge and the Ganter Bridge.

EXAMPLE 6-2

Determine the present worth of the following cash flow diagram and an 8% interest rate. (Notice how the gradient starts in year 2.)

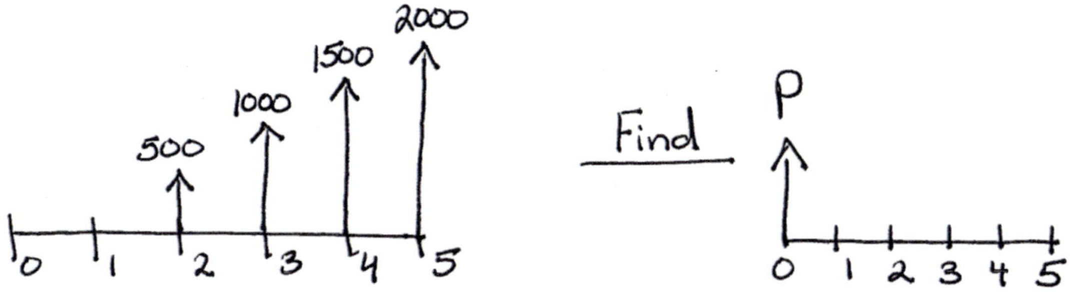

$$P = G\left[\frac{(1+i)^n - in - 1}{i^2(1+i)^n}\right] = 500\left[\frac{(1+0.08)^5 - 0.08(5) - 1}{(0.08)^2(1+0.08)^5}\right]$$

$$P = \$3686.21$$

"[John] Kobak explained, 'The way you learn anything is that something fails, and you figure out how not to have it fail again." — Robert S. Arrighi, Pursuit of Power: NASA's Propulsion Systems

EXAMPLE 6-3

What is the Present Worth of the cash flow diagram given below using an annual interest rate of 5%?

Solution: I used the arithmetic graidient present worth formula to move the cash flow to year two, then moved the value at year two to year zero. Be careful combining equations!

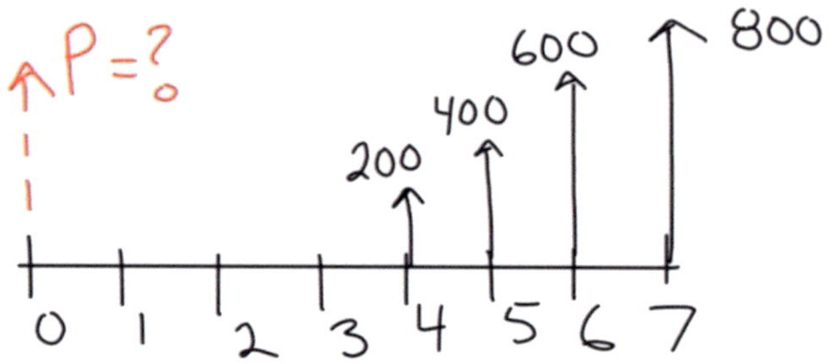

P_2 - present value year 2

$$P_2 = G\left[\frac{(1+i)^n - in - 1}{i^2(1+i)^n}\right]$$ ← move cash to time P_2

$$P_0 = F(1+i)^{-n} = P_2(1+i)^{-n}$$ ← move P_2 to P_0

$$P = P_2 \times P_0 = G\left[\frac{(1+i)^n - in - 1}{i^2(1+i)^n}\right](1+i)^{-n}$$

$$P = 200\left[\frac{(1+0.05)^5 - 0.05(5) - 1}{0.05^2(1+0.05)^5}\right](1+0.05)^{-2} = \$1494.23$$

EXAMPLE 6-4

If the present worth at time ∅ (zero) is equal to ∅ (zero) using an 8% interest rate, what is the value of N?

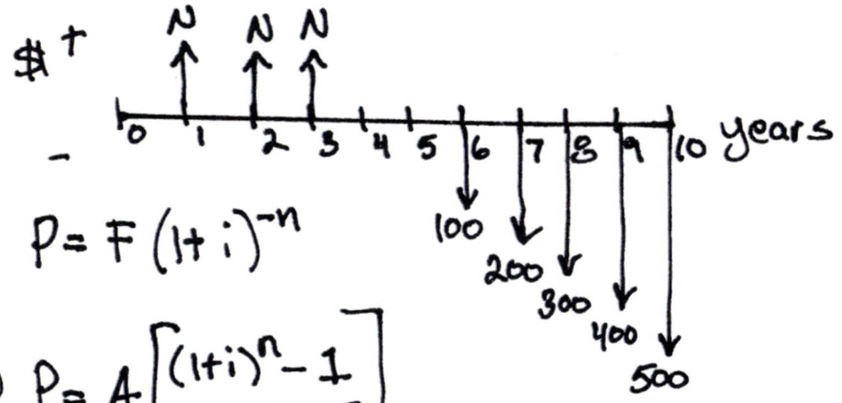

① $P = F(1+i)^{-n}$

② $P = A\left[\dfrac{(1+i)^n - 1}{i(1+i)^n}\right]$

③ $P = G\left[\dfrac{(1+i)^n - in - 1}{i^2(1+i)^n}\right]$

$$PW = N\left[\frac{(1+.08)^3 - 1}{.08(1+.08)^3}\right] + \underbrace{\left[100\left[\frac{(1+.08)^6 - .08(6) - 1}{.08^2(1+.08)^6}\right]\right]}_{F_4}\underbrace{(1+.08)^{-4}}_{(1+i)^{-n}}$$

$= \underline{\underline{0}}$ solve for N

$N = \underline{\underline{\$300.14}}$

3) GEOMETRIC GRADIENT - UNIFORM RATE

A geometric gradient is simply a uniform rate (percentage) change between interest periods, it can be positive or negative, it can grow upward or be diminishing downward.

In the figure below, a increasing gradient is shown where A_1 is the value in the first time period. The subsequent values are based on the first value, A_1. For example, $A_2 = A_1 + (A_1 * g)$, $A_3 = A_2 + (A_2 * g)$, where g is the percentage change.

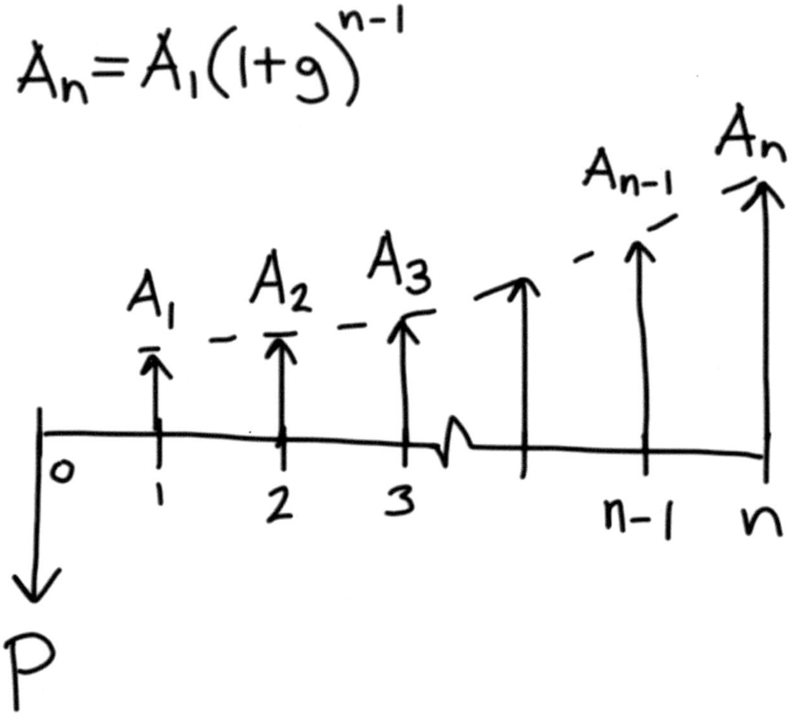

Two cases can occur with geometric gradients, 1) the interest rate equals the gradient, and 2) the interest rate does not equal the gradient. The formulas for the two cases are given below.

g – uniform gradient benefit or cost amount
A_1 – first interest period value
i – Interest rate per period
n – Number of interest periods
P – Present Worth

Geometric Gradient

Case 1 - Interest rate equals gradient rate.

$$P = A_1 n(1+i)^{-1}$$ **when i=g.**

Case 2 - Interest rate does not equal gradient rate.

$$P = A_1\left[\frac{1-(1+g)^n(1+i)^{-1}}{i-g}\right]$$ **when i is not equal to g.**

Famous Engineers you should know!

Karl von Terzaghi

(October 2, 1883– October 25, 1963)

Teraghi was an Austrian engineer considered the father of Soil mechanics.

From Wikipedia

The American Society of Civil Engineers established in 1960 the Karl Terzaghi Award to an "author of outstanding contributions to knowledge in the fields of soil mechanics, subsurface and earthwork engineering, and subsurface and earthwork construction".

EXAMPLE 6-4

You wrote an app for the ipad that helps kids learn structural analysis (good on you). Assume you make $2000 in the first year and your profit will grow at a rate of 9% per year. At an interest rate of 9% , what is the present worth of your first five years in the app world.

Case 1.

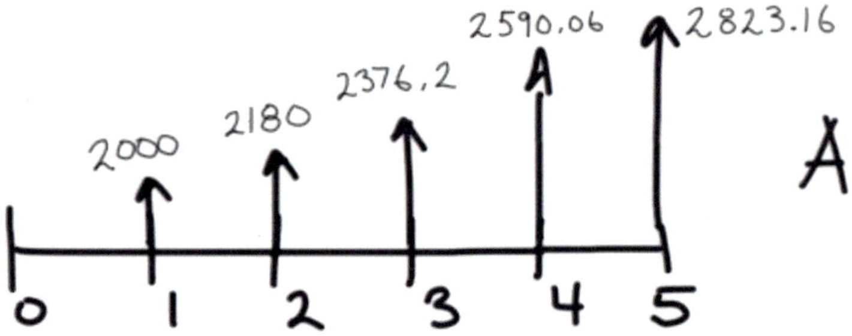

$$A_n = A_1 (1+g)^{n-1}$$

$$= 2000(1+0.09)^4$$

$$= \underline{\underline{2823.16}}$$

Since $i = g$

$$P = A_1 n (1+i)^{-1}$$

$$P = 2000(5)(1.09)^{-1} = \underline{\underline{\$9174.31}}$$

EXAMPLE 6-5

A cash flow begins at $10,000 the first year, with a 10% annual increase until n=10 years. If the interest rate is 7%, what is the present value of the cash flow?

Case 2.

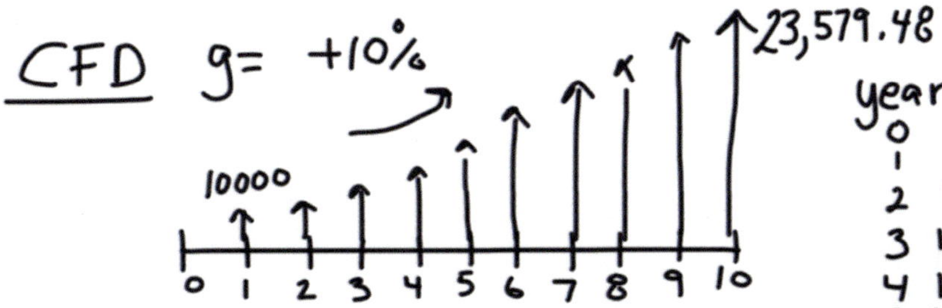

year	Value
0	0
1	10,000
2	11,000
3	12,100
4	13,310
5	14,641
6	16,105.10
7	17,715.61
8	19,487.17
9	21,435.89
10	23,579.48

$i \neq g$

$$P = A_1\left[\frac{1-(1+g)^n(1+i)^{-n}}{i-g}\right]$$

$$P = 10000\left[\frac{1-(1+0.1)^{10}(1+0.07)^{-10}}{0.07-0.10}\right] = \$106{,}175.71$$

CHAPTER 7 - CONTINUOUS COMPOUNDING

1) CONTINUOUS COMPOUNDING – SINGLE VALUE FORMULAS

Continuous compounding is just what it sounds like, the interest time period becomes infinitesimally small, and the interest rate is compounded over the small time period. It seems the main use of continuous compounding is in the stock market and use as an easy equation to get a quick result.

r = nominal interest rate per year
m = number of compounding sub-periods per year
r/m = interest rate per interest period
mn = number of compounding sub-periods in n years

Derivation of Continuous Compounding:

$$F = P(1+i)^n = P\left(1+\frac{r}{m}\right)^{mn}$$

for continuous compounding $m \Rightarrow \infty$

from Calculus (famous limit)

$$\lim_{x \to 0} (1+x)^{1/x} = 2.71828 = e$$

let $x = \frac{r}{m} \Rightarrow m = \frac{r}{x} \Rightarrow mn$ becomes $\frac{rn}{x}$ or $rn\left(\frac{1}{x}\right)$

Substituting the limit into the formula,

$$F = P\left[\lim_{x \to 0} (1+x)^{1/x}\right]^{rn} = Pe^{rn}$$

Continuous Compounding formulas

$F = Pe^{rn}$ (Future Worth)

$P = Fe^{-rn}$ (Present Worth)

$i_a = e^r - 1$ (effective interest - continuous compound)

EXAMPLE 7-1

Find the future worth of $2000 dollars, at a 7% nominal interest rate, in 5 years.

a) If the interest is compounded yearly
b) If the interest is compounded monthly
c) If the interest rate is compounded daily
d) If the interest rate is compounded continuously
e) What is the effective yearly interest based on continuous compounding?

a) $F = P\left(1+\frac{r}{m}\right)^{mn} = 2000\left(1+\frac{0.07}{1}\right)^{1(5)}$

$= \$2805.10$

b) $F = P\left(1+\frac{r}{m}\right)^{mn} = 2000\left(1+\frac{0.07}{12}\right)^{12(5)}$

$= \$2835.25$

c) $F = P\left(1+\frac{r}{m}\right)^{mn} = 2000\left(1+\frac{0.07}{365}\right)^{365(5)}$

$= \$2838.04$

d) $F = Pe^{rn} = 2000(2.71828)^{0.07(5)}$

$= \$2838.14$

e) $i_a = e^r - 1 = (2.71828)^{0.07} - 1 = 0.0725$

$= 7.25\%$

EXAMPLE 7-2

Your local bank pays 5% nominal interest on checking accounts. What is the effective annual interest rate if interest is compounded,

a) Every 4 months?
b) Daily?
c) Continuously?

a) $i_a = \left(1+\frac{r}{m}\right)^m - 1 = \left(1+\frac{0.05}{3}\right)^3 - 1$

$= 0.0508 = \underline{\underline{5.08\%}}$

b) $i_a = \left(1+\frac{r}{m}\right)^m - 1 = \left(1+\frac{0.05}{365}\right)^{365} - 1$

$= 0.051267 = \underline{\underline{5.13\%}}$

c) $i_a = e^r - 1 = (e)^{0.05} - 1$

$= 0.05127 = \underline{\underline{5.13\%}}$

EXAMPLE 7-3

How much would you have to invest today to receive $10,000 in 4.5 years, at a nominal interest rate of 9%, based on continuous compounding?

$$P = Fe^{-rn} = 10000(e)^{-0.09(4.5)}$$

$$= \$6,669.77$$

"If you owe your bank a hundred pounds, you have a problem. But if you owe a million, it has."

— John Maynard Keynes

CHAPTER 8 – INTERNAL RATE OF RETURN

1) INTERNAL RATE OF RETURN OVERVIEW

An Internal Rate of Return (IRR) analysis is one of the most used tools in the economic community. An IRR calculation helps to evaluate the desirability of a project or investment. (The term *internal* refers to the fact that its calculation does not incorporate environmental factors (e.g., inflation).)

The official definition goes something like this, the Internal Rate of Return is the interest rate that makes the Net Present Value (NPV) equal to zero. It is essentially the interest rate at which the investment breaks even.

In equation form, Net present value (NPV) = Net Present Worth Benefits (P_B) – Net Present Worth Costs (P_C) = 0

One more term we have to define is the MARR or **Minimum Attractive Rate of Rate**. The Minimum Attractive Rate of Return is exactly what it sounds like, the minimum return (%) that an investor would consider on an investment.

For example, say you have invested your money in a construction company and you were hoping for a 10% return on your money. This is considered the MARR for your investment. (Banks typical pay 2-3% return on your money in a savings account) When you check the IRR of your investment you find that your money is actually making a 20% return on your money and it's time to buy that boat you always wanted.

2) FINDING THE INTERNAL RATE OF RETURN FOR ONE ALTERNATIVE

For evaluating one investment or economic alternative,

MARR < IRR – great investment
MARR = IRR – the minimum return you will accept, good investment
MARR > IRR – reject the investment, it does not meet your minimum return requirements

EXAMPLE 8-1

You invested \$3,000 dollars in a mutual fund today. You are hoping to make at least a 10% return on your money. At the end of five years you cash out of the fund and realize a payout of \$8,000 on your initial investment. What is the Rate of return on your investment?

Solution: You are looking for the interest rate that will make your benefits minus your costs equal to zero, evaluated at the same point in time (typically the present). $P_B - P_C = 0$. Interest rate when this occurs is the internal rate of return (IRR)

MARR = 10%

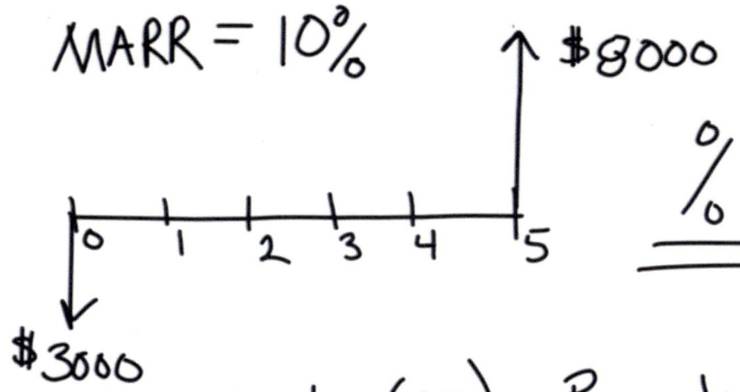

%?

net Present Value (NPV) = Present Worth Benefits (P_B) − Present Worth Costs (P_C) = 0

or

$0 = P_B - P_C$ ⇒ find interest rate (IRR)

$0 = F(1+i)^{-n} - 3000$

$0 = 8000(1+i)^{-5} - 3000$

find i → from Calculator solver

$i = IRR = 0.217$

or 21.7% > 10% ✓ good

8-1 cont. A graph of the problem 9-1, Present Worth vs. Interest Rate. (At 0% interest, PW = \$8000-\$3000 = \$5000)

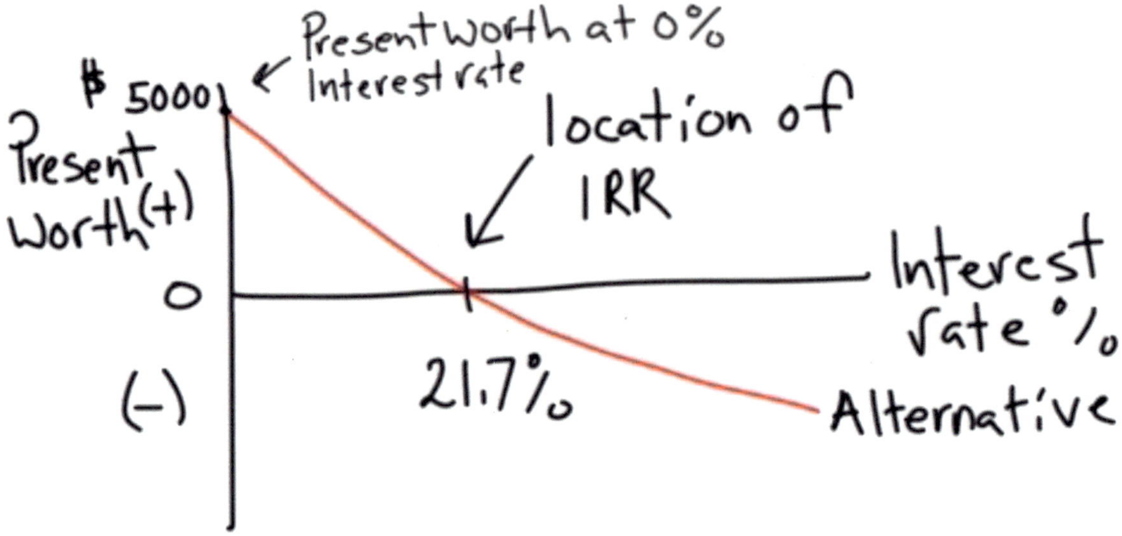

"Economics is extremely useful as a form of employment for economists."

— John Kenneth Galbraith

EXAMPLE 8-2

You received a $2000 dollar loan from a bank, with a repayment schedule of $500 per year for 7 years. What interest rate are you paying on the loan? Use a graphical rate of return analysis to find the IRR.

Solution: Develop a graph of Net Present Worth vs. i, Interest Rate and find where the NPW = 0. That will be the interest rate where benefits = costs.

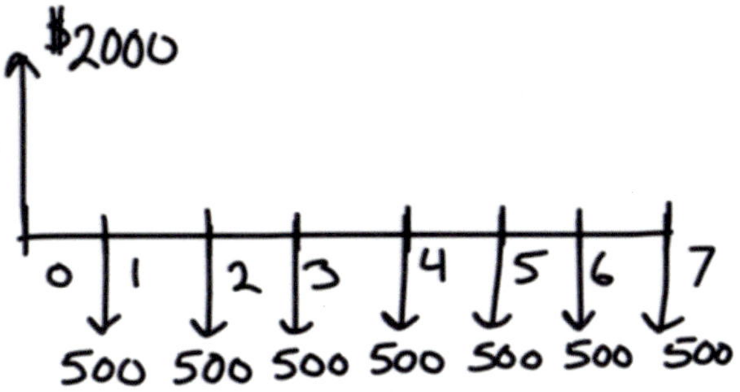

i%	NPW
0	-1500
5	-893.19
10	-434.21
15	-80.21
20	197.70
25	419.43

$$NPW = A\left[\frac{(1+i)^n - 1}{i(1+i)^n}\right]$$

ie) $i = 10\%$

$$NPW = -500\left[\frac{(1+0.1)^7 - 1}{0.1(1+0.1)^7}\right]$$

$$= -434.21$$

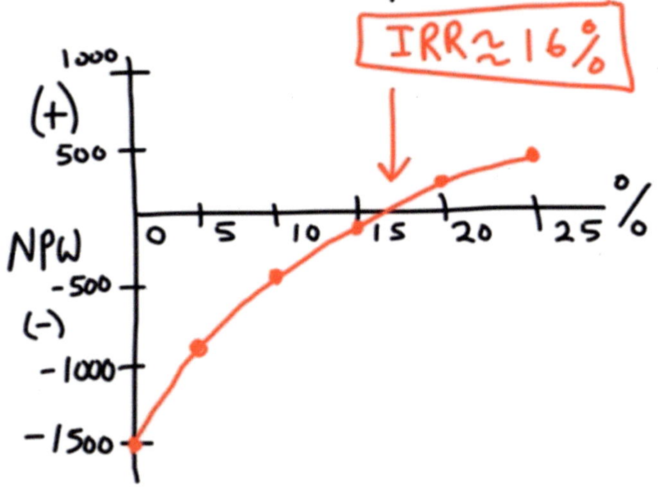

8-2 cont. You are paying an interest rate of 16% on the loan. Notice how the graphs look for different cash flows.

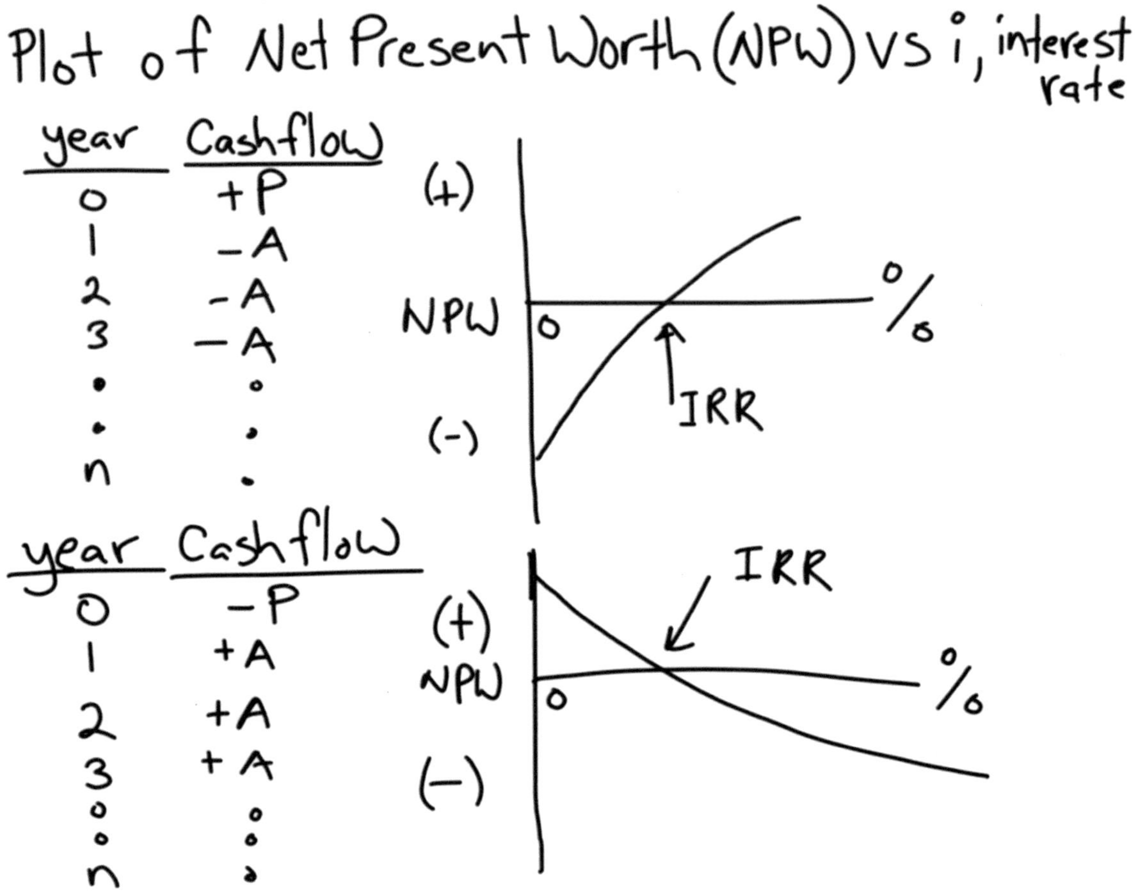

"99 percent of all statistics only tell 49 percent of the story."

— Ron DeLegge II, Gents with No Cents

3) INTERNAL RATE OF RETURN EVALUATING MULTIPLE ALTERNATIVES

When you have multiple economic alternatives to compare you can use the Internal Rate of Return analysis to find the most desirable alternative. An IRR calculation also has the added benefit of locating the interest rate regions where each alternative gives you the best return. (A single alternative is typically not the best for all rates of returns.)

For comparing two alternatives, you can do hand calculations, using an Incremental Rate of Return ΔIRR to find the interest rate where they cross or meet. When you are comparing more than two alternatives you should consider using Excel or a similar spreadsheet package.

Incremental Rate of Return (ΔIRR)

Take the higher first cost alternative minus the lower first cost alternative and find the ΔIRR for this new cash flow diagram. The ΔIRR is the interest rate point that both alternatives have in common, a point where they both meet on a Present Worth vs. Interest rate graph.

Steps for evaluating multiple alternatives

1) Determine the IRR of each alternative to see if they meet or exceed the MARR. Discard the ones that do not meet MARR.
2) Graph all the remaining alternatives, from step 1), on a Present Worth vs. Interest Rate chart. The interest rate where the alternatives cross the zero present worth axis is their IRR.
3) Use incremental rate of return between alternatives to find the exact interest where they cross.
4) Make a choice table, showing which alternative is most desirable for different interest rates.

Choice Table (See examples and video example)

A choice table is used to show which alternative is best in different regions on a Present worth vs. Interest rate graph. The higher Present Worth determines the better alternative. (See figure)

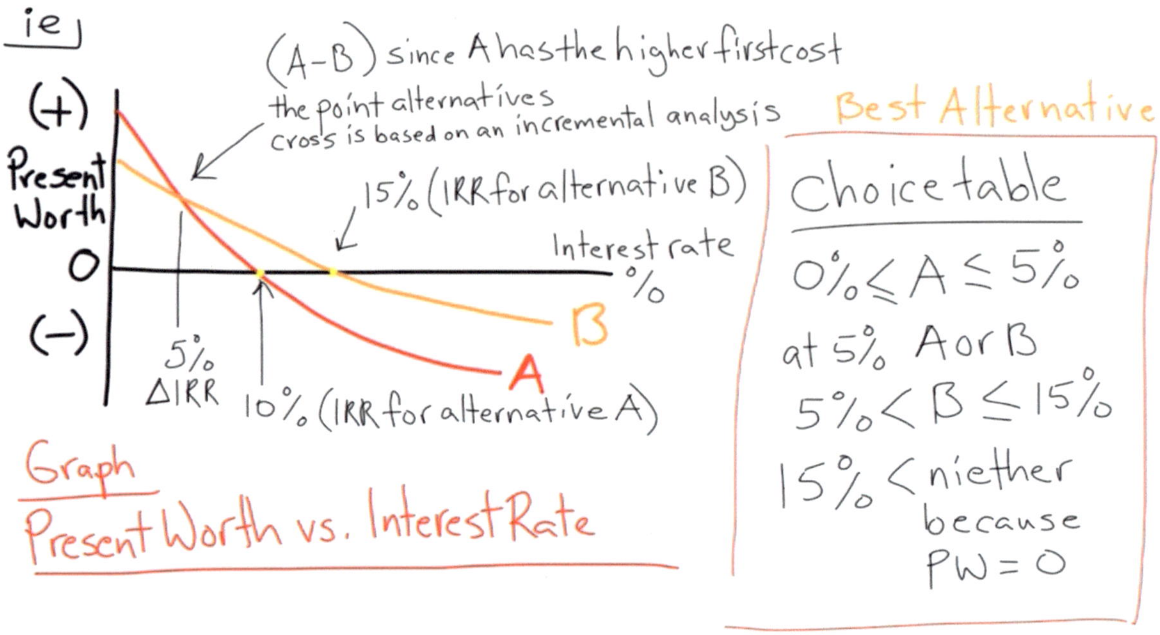

"An economist is an expert who will know tomorrow why the things he predicted yesterday didn't happen today."

— Laurence J. Peter

EXAMPLE 8-3

Two alternatives are being considered for a new crane. Using a MARR of 7% and an eight year analysis period, if identical replacement is assumed, which alternative should be selected based on a rate of return analysis? Solution: Note when you have alternatives with unequal lives, you can pick a common denominator (number of years) and repeat the cash flows assuming the costs stay the same but are repeated.

	Crane A	Crane B
Initial cost	\$9400	\$5200
Uniform annual benefit	\$1750	\$1650
Useful life in years	8	4

To find IRR set Net Present Worth = 0 ⇒ Benefits = Costs

CFD

Crane A

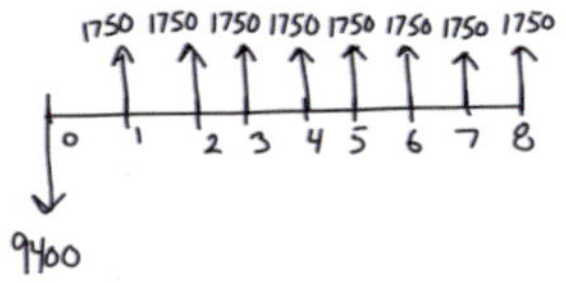

Crane B (double the life)

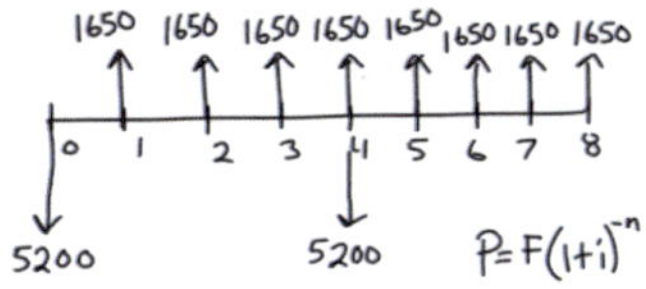

$P = F(1+i)^{-n}$ $P = A\left[\frac{(1+i)^n - 1}{i(1+i)^n}\right]$

Ⓐ Find IRR Benefits = costs

$$A\left[\frac{(1+i)^n - 1}{i(1+i)^n}\right] = \text{Present Cost}$$

$$1750\left[\frac{(1+i)^8 - 1}{i(1+i)^8}\right] = 9400$$

Trial & error ⇒ input i = 5, 6, 7 etc or calculator solver

$i = 9.81\%$

IRR = 9.81% > 7% ok ✓

Ⓑ

$$NPW = 0 = \text{Present cost} + F(1+i)^{-n} + A\left[\frac{(1+i)^n - 1}{i(1+i)^n}\right]$$

$$0 = -5200 + -5200(1+i)^{-4} + 1650\left[\frac{(1+i)^8 - 1}{i(1+i)^8}\right]$$

Solving for i

$i = 10.27\%$ ✓

IRR = 10.27% > 7% ok

Both alternatives are acceptable, need incremental analysis to determine "best" alternative.

(A–B) higher first cost − lower first cost

CFD

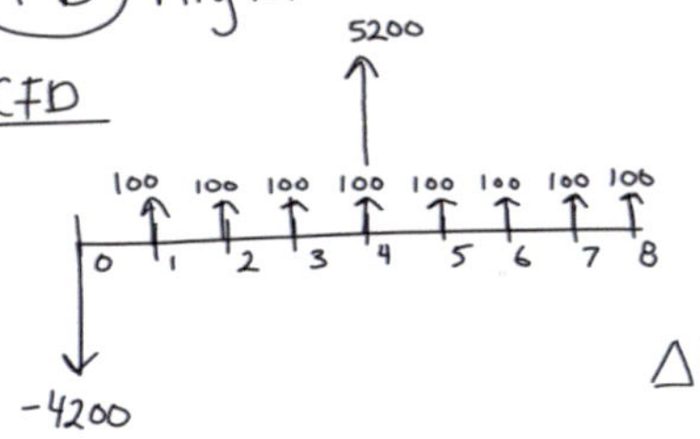

First Cost

$P = F(1+i)^{-n}$ $P = A\left[\frac{(1+i)^n - 1}{i(1+i)^n}\right]$

$$NPW = 0 = -4200 + 5200(1+i)^{-4} + 100\left[\frac{(1+i)^8 - 1}{i(1+i)^8}\right]$$

$i = 9.24\% > 7\%$

ΔIRR = 9.24% Choose A

EXAMPLE 8-4

Solving Example 8-3 with Excel. To find the Internal Rate of Return (IRR) in Excel, you use the formula =IRR(value1, value2, value3, etc..).

In the chart on the right, instead of solving for i (interest rate), I found the present worth of each alternative at different interest rates and graphed the results. From there you can see where each alternative crosses the zero present worth axis, which is the location of the IRR of the alternative.

Notice where the two alternatives cross, at 9.24%, which is the IRR of the Incremental (ΔIRR) analysis (A-B).

Choice Table

Pick Alternative A from 0% to 9.24%
Pick Alternative B from 9.24% to 10.27%
Pick neither after 10.27% interest because all present worth values become negative.

year	Crane A	Crane B	A-B
0	-9400	-5200	-4200
1	1750	1650	100
2	1750	1650	100
3	1750	1650	100
4	1750	-3550	5300
5	1750	1650	100
6	1750	1650	100
7	1750	1650	100
8	1750	1650	100
IRR =	9.81%	10.27%	9.24%

Interest Rate	Present Worth Crane A	Present Worth Crane B
0	$4,600.00	$2,800.00
2	$3,419.59	$2,083.05
4	$2,382.30	$1,464.05
6	$1,467.14	$927.27
8	$656.62	$459.80
9.24	$200.13	$200.01
10	($63.88)	$50.96
12	($706.63)	($308.09)
14	($1,281.99)	($624.69)

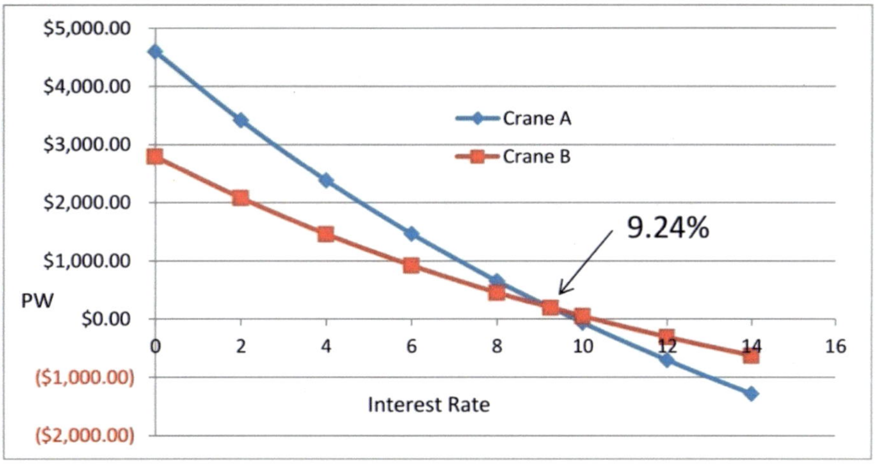

EXAMPLE 8-5

A contractor is considering whether to buy or lease a forklift for her precast plant. Which option should she take (A or B) based on a MARR = 12% and a,

a) A Present Worth analysis
b) A Annual Cash Flow analysis
c) A Rate of Return analysis

Options / year	(Buy) Alternative A	(lease) Alternative B	Incremental (A-B)
0	\$ -11,000	\$ -2,300	\$ -8,700
1		\$ -2,300	\$ +2,300
2		\$ -2,300	\$ +2,300
3		\$ -2,300	\$ +2,300
4		\$ -2,300	\$ +2,300
5		\$ -2,300	\$ +2,300
6		\$ -2,300	\$ +2,300

Ⓐ CFD

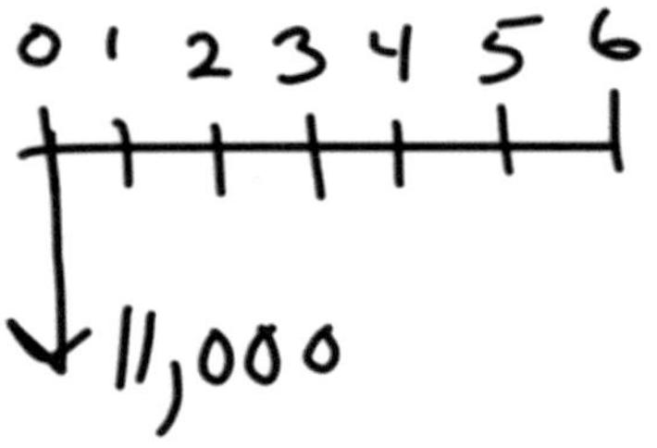

Ⓑ CFD

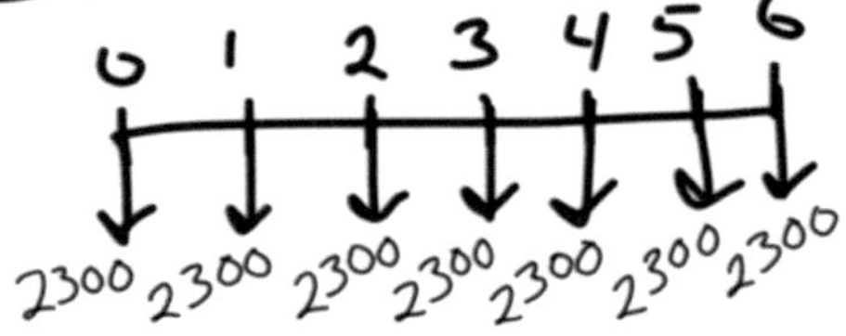

8-5 cont.

a) Present Worth

(A) $PW = \$^{-}11{,}000$

(B) $PW_B = {}^{-}2500 + A\left[\frac{(1+i)^n - 1}{i(1+i)^n}\right] = {}^{-}2500 + {}^{-}2500\left[\frac{(1+.12)^6 - 1}{.12(1+.12)^6}\right]$

$PW_B = {}^{-}11{,}756.24$

choose (A) — lower first cost

b) Annual Cashflow Analysis

(A) $A = P\left[\frac{i(1+i)^n}{(1+i)^n - 1}\right]$

$A = {}^{-}11{,}000\left[\frac{0.12(1+.12)^6}{(1+.12)^6 - 1}\right] = \$^{-}2675.48$

(B) $A = P\left[\frac{i(1+i)^n}{(1+i)^n - 1}\right] + {}^{-}2500$ ← already annual payment

$A = {}^{-}2500\left[\frac{.12(1+.12)^6}{(1+.12)^6 - 1}\right] + {}^{-}2500$

$A_B = \$^{-}3108.06$

choose A — lower annual cost (payment)

"One of the greatest pieces of economic wisdom is to know what you do not know."

— John Kenneth Galbraith

Example 8-5 cont. Because of the negative cash flows finding which alternative is better at a particular interest rate is best found through the use of a graph. The Incremental Rate of Return ΔIRR, shows where the interest rate where the two alternatives cross. Finding the present worth of the alternatives at different interest rates allows you to draw a graph of present worth vs. interest rate.

c) Rate of Return Analysis

This is a little tricky because of the cost only cash flow diagrams.

Start with ΔIRR of incremental CFD (A-B)

NPV = 0 = Benefits - costs = 0 (use Present Worth to evaluate)

$$A\left[\frac{(1+i)^n-1}{i(1+i)^n}\right]-8700=0$$

Draw a graph

$$2300\left[\frac{(1+i)^6-1}{i(1+i)^6}\right]-8700=0$$

$\Delta IRR = 15\%$ (Calculator)

↗ interest rate where alternatives cross

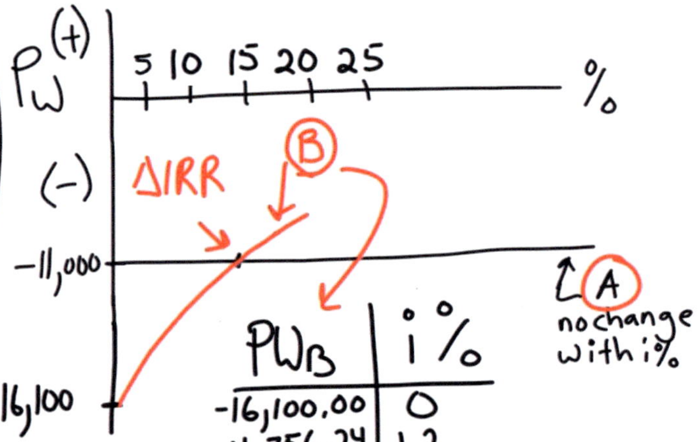

PW_B	i%
-16,100.00	0
-11,756.24	12
-11,000	15
-9,948	20

@15% or less interest

Choose (A)

Note that alternative B would be preferred at interest rates over 15% and A is preferred for any rate under 15%. Also note that no matter what analysis system you use you should always get the same alternative winning.

CHAPTER 9 – ECONOMIC EQUIVALENCE

Economic equivalence is based on the idea that economically speaking, money can have the same value at different times. For example, if you won $10,000 today, this is exactly the same amount of money as $21,589.25, ten years from now based on a 8% nominal interest rate. It is just moved to a different time period. The two sums are exactly the same as long as the interest rate does not change. Equivalence exists between cash flows that have the same economic effect and could therefore be traded for one another.

Example: $10,000 today is economically equal to $21,589.25 ten years from now at 8% interest.

$F=P(1+i)^n$

$F= \$10,000(1+0.08)^{10} = \$21,589.25$

Economic equivalence is dependent on a stable interest rate. As long as the rate stays the same over the analysis, cash flows can be moved anywhere along a timeline and still be ECONOMICALLY equivalent.

This is a very helpful concept when you are choosing between different alternatives. Often times by moving cash flows to identical locations in time, for comparison, it is relatively easy to determine which alternative is the better value.

Famous Engineers you should know!

Eugene C. Figg

(August 4, 1936 – March 20, 2002)

Mr. Figg was an American structural engineer who made numerous contributions to the field of structural engineering, especially in the design of the cable-stayed bridge and the use of the segmental concrete construction method.

EXAMPLE 9-1

Compute the equivalent value of S, by moving the series of $1000, and assuming a 12% interest rate. Solution: The question asks you to move the three $1000 cash flows to a different location on a timeline. This is what economic equivalence is all about, the series of "S" values is equivalent to the series of $1000, as long as the interest rate stays the same throughout the timeline.

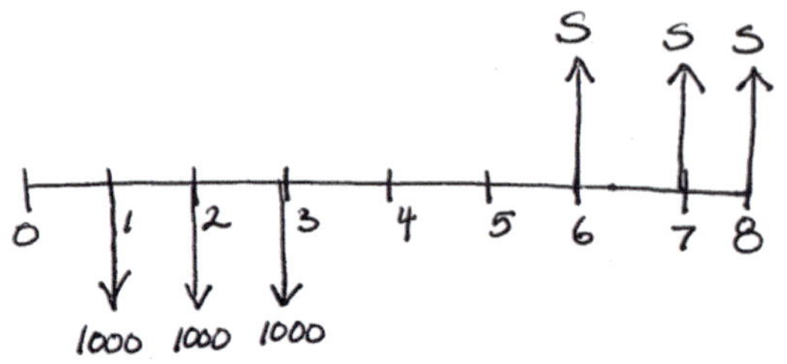

Steps – you can move the money anywhere on the timeline as long as your take in to account the interest rate.

One Method

Move money to Ø.

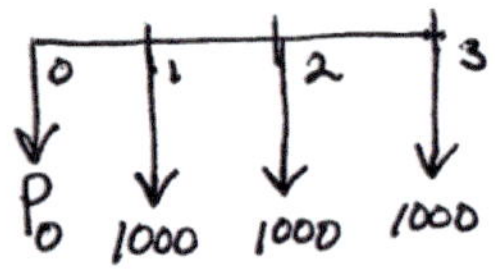

$$P_0 = A\left[\frac{(1+i)^n - 1}{i(1+i)^n}\right] = 1000\left[\frac{(1+0.12)^3 - 1}{0.12(1+0.12)^3}\right]$$

$$P_0 = 2401.83$$

move money to year 5

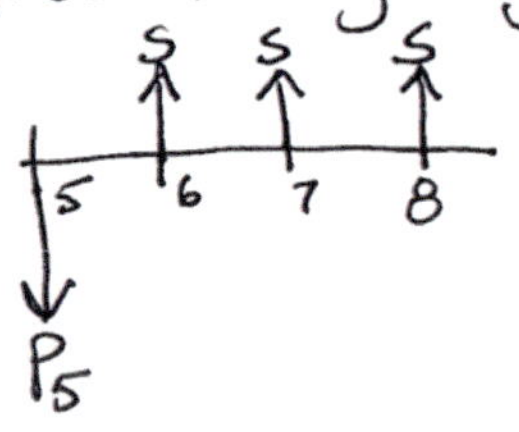

$$P_5 = F(1+i)^{-n} = 2401.83(1+0.12)^{-5}$$

$$P_5 = 1362.86$$

$$S = A = P\left[\frac{i(1+i)^n}{(1+i)^n - 1}\right] = 1362.86\left[\frac{0.12(1+0.12)^3}{(1+0.12)^3 - 1}\right]$$

$$S = A = \$567.43$$

EXAMPLE 9-2

Compute the equivalent lump sum amount at n=3, for V, using a 10% annual interest rate for the cash flow shown below.

Solution: Move all the values in years 0 to 2 forward, and years 4 to 5 backwards to year 3. The $150 in year 3 just stays there.

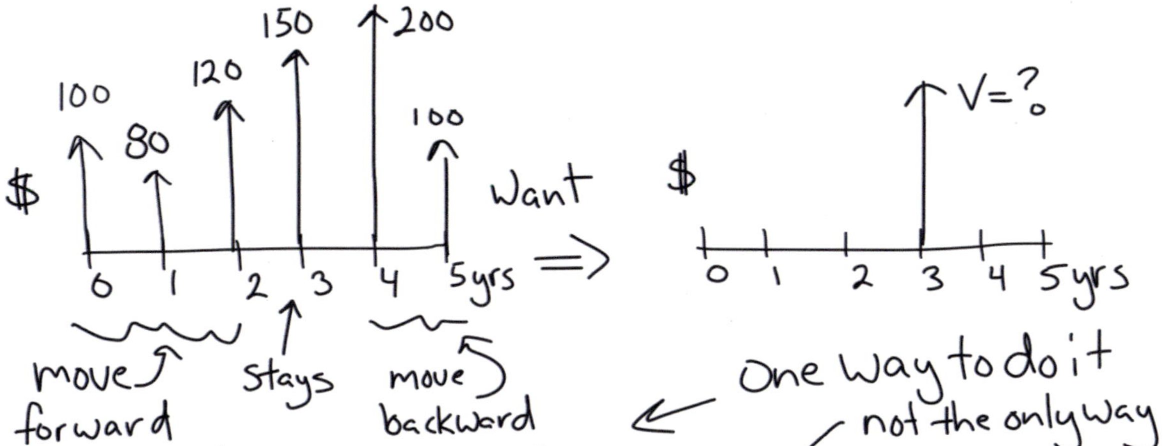

$F = P(1+i)^{n}$ $\quad P = F(1+i)^{-n}$

$$V = 100(1+0.1)^{3} + 80(1+0.1)^{2} + 120(1+0.1)^{1} + 150$$

$$+ 200(1+0.1)^{-1} + 100(1+0.1)^{-2} = \underline{\$776.36}$$

In economic equivalence, both cash flows diagrams are the same and "equal" at 10% annual interest.

EXAMPLE 9-3

Given i = 9%, find the values of B (CFD 2) that make the following two cash flows (1 and 2) economically equivalent. (Note: They are many ways to solve the problem, I just showed one possible solution.)

Solution: This is a favorite problem for instructors, something that looks hard but turns out to be pretty easy. In this case we can find the value of the two cash flow diagrams at a common point, V_2 (CFD 3), and then set them equal to solve for B.

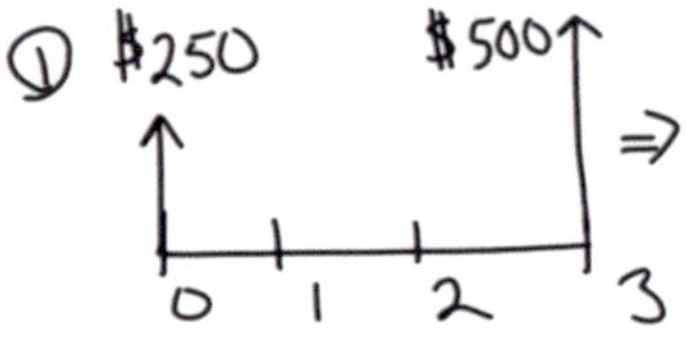

using $F = P(1+i)^n$ & $P = F(1+i)^{-n}$

$$\Rightarrow V_2 = 250(1+0.09)^2 + 500(1+0.09)^{-1} = \underline{\underline{755.74}}$$

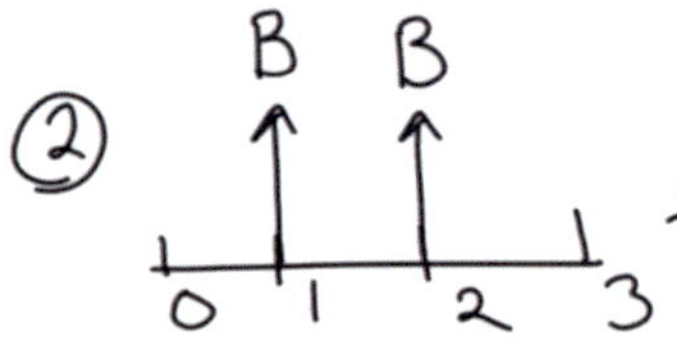

$$\Rightarrow V_2 = B(1+0.09)^1 + B = \underline{\underline{2.09B}}$$

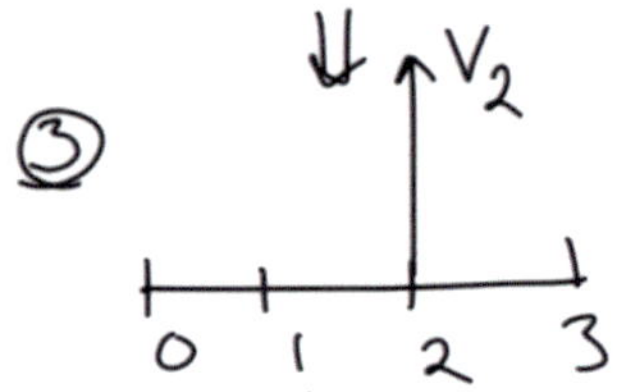

Set ① & ② equal solve for B.

$$\Rightarrow V_{2_1} = V_{2_2}$$

$$755.74 = 2.09B$$

$$B = \underline{\underline{361.60}}$$

EXAMPLE 9-4

At what interest rate would cash flow A be equal to cash flow B? (Economic equivalency is dependent on the interest rate!)

Solution: Pick a point on the timeline and set the two cash flows equal at this point. In this case find the value of both CFDs at time zero or present worth.

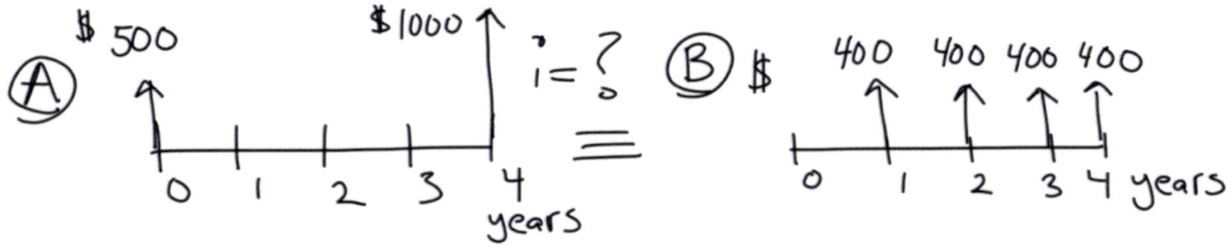

Pick a common time point to evaluate each CFD

Use time Ø (Present Worth)

(A) $P_A = 500 + F(1+i)^{-4} = 500 + 1000(1+i)^{-4}$

$$P_B = A\left[\frac{(1+i)^n - 1}{i(1+i)^n}\right]$$

$$P_B = 400\left[\frac{(1+i)^4 - 1}{i(1+i)^4}\right]$$

Set $P_A = P_B$ solve for i

$$500 + 1000(1+i)^{-4} = 400\left[\frac{(1+i)^4 - 1}{i(1+i)^4}\right]$$

$$i = 0.343 = 34.3\%$$

CHAPTER 10 – BENEFIT COST RATIOS

1) BENEFIT-COST RATIOS

Typically, when you are evaluating whether or not an alternative is desirable, (makes money) you determine the net worth of the cash flow at some point in time. If the net worth is positive, the alternative is economically attractive. Obviously if the net worth is negative it is an alternative not worth pursuing.

Net worth = Benefits (at a chosen point in time) – Costs (at the same chosen point in time)

If you set the net worth to zero, the equation becomes,

Benefits = Costs, which leads to Benefits/Costs = 1.

If the ratio of Benefits/Costs = 1 than you are not making money but you are also not losing money, it is the break-even point. So if the benefit/cost ratio is greater than zero, you are making money, less than zero, you are losing money.

You can evaluate the Benefit/Cost ratio at any point on the cash flow timeline as long as both values (B & C) are determined at the same point. Usually they are evaluated at the beginning of the timeline (time zero) or at the end of the timeline (Time = n).

Famous Engineers you should know!

Tung-Yen Lin

(November 4,1912 – November 15, 2003)

T.Y. Lin was a structural engineer who was the pioneer of standardizing the use of prestressed concrete. Lin fought against the pressures of economy by incorporating more aesthetics into his bridges and developing new techniques that increased economy. Lin believed that "engineering approach should be a global vision of the bridge.

EXAMPLE 10-1

For the cash flow given below, determine if it is an acceptable alternative based on a benefit/cost ratio. The interest rate is 4.5%. (P_B = present worth of benefit, P_C = present worth of cost.)

CFD B/C ratio

Find P of benefits

P of costs

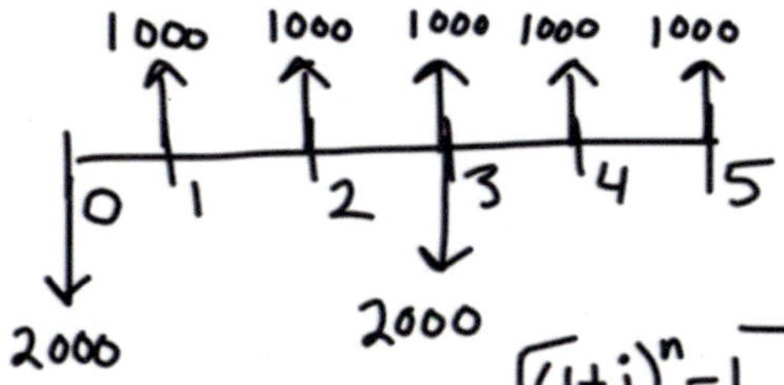

$$\frac{B}{C} = \frac{P_B}{P_C} = \frac{A\left[\frac{(1+i)^n-1}{i(1+i)^n}\right]}{2000+F(1+i)^{-n}} = \frac{1000\left[\frac{(1+0.045)^5-1}{0.045(1+0.045)^5}\right]}{2000+2000(1+0.045)^{-3}}$$

↑ year 3

$$\frac{B}{C} = \frac{4389.98}{3752.59} = \underline{\underline{1.17}} \geq 1 \checkmark \text{good}$$

You can see the present worth of the benefit is higher than the present worth of the cost, so B/C>1.

2) INCREMENTAL BENEFIT-COST RATIO

When you are comparing Benefit/Cost ratios between alternatives, you cannot rely on the individual B/C values. For example, suppose you are evaluating two alternatives using B/C ratios. Alternative A has a B/C = 1.2 and Alternative B has a B/C = 1.3. Alternative B is not automatically the better choice because it has a higher B/C value. This could be due to higher cash flow values in one of the alternatives.

Since both alternatives have a B/C > 1 they are both acceptable alternatives, to find the more desirable choice you have to calculate an incremental Benefit-Cost ratio.

To calculate an Incremental B/C ratio, you take the alternative with the higher first cost and subtract the values of the lower first cost alternative and then calculate a B/C ratio for the difference in values between the two alternatives. If the incremental B/C > 1, then the higher first cost alternative is the preferred choice. If the incremental B/C < 1, then the lower first cost alternative is the more desirable alternative.

Incremental Analysis Two Alternatives

First check both alternatives have a B/C > 1, then find the incremental cash flow (Higher first cost minus the lower first cost)

B/C > 1 – Choose higher first cost alternative
B/C < 1 – Choose the lower first cost alternative
B/C = 1 – both alternatives are equal (but neither one is making money)

If you have more than two alternatives, you will have to calculate more than one incremental benefit/cost ratio.

Incremental Analysis More than two alternatives

Check all alternatives to see which ones have a B/C > 1, discard those alternatives that do not. For the remaining alternatives that do have a B/C >1, calculate an incremental analysis between two alternatives, picking the winner of the two and then comparing the winner to the next alternative. Continue until all alternatives have been compared.

B/C > 1 – Choose higher first cost alternative
B/C < 1 – Choose the lower first cost alternative
B/C = 1 – both alternatives are equal (but neither one is making money)

EXAMPLE 10-2

Based on a benefit/cost ratio, which of the two alternatives given below should be chosen? Use an interest rate of 9% for the analysis. **Hint**: First check both alternatives have a benefit/cost ratio greater or equal to one and then calculate an incremental benefit/cost ratio. (Note the formulas used for determining present worth, in this example, may not always be the same ones as shown below.)

Benefit Cost Analysis $i = 9\%$

	A	B	Incremental B−A
First Cost	\$3500	\$5000	5000−3500 = \$1500
Uniform annual benefit	\$1050	\$1800	1800 −1050 = \$750
useful life, years	5	5	

① check alternatives both meet B/C > 1

Ⓐ $\frac{\text{Present worth benefits}}{\text{Present worth costs}} = \frac{B}{C} = \frac{A\left[\frac{(1+i)^n-1}{i(1+i)^n}\right]}{\text{First cost}} = \frac{1050\left[\frac{(1+0.09)^5-1}{0.09(1+0.09)^5}\right]}{3500}$

$B/C = \frac{4084.13}{3500} = 1.17 > 1$ OK✓

Ⓑ $B/C = \frac{A\left[\frac{(1+i)^n-1}{i(1+i)^n}\right]}{\text{First cost}} = \frac{1800\left[\frac{(1+0.09)^5-1}{0.09(1+0.09)^5}\right]}{5000} = \frac{7001.37}{5000} = 1.4 > 1$ OK✓

Both alternatives are good, now check incremental (B−A) to determine the "best" alternative.

(B−A) $B/C = \frac{750\left[\frac{(1+0.09)^5}{0.09(1+0.09)^5}\right]}{1500} = \frac{2917.24}{1500} = 1.94 > 1$

Since B/C of the incremental (B−A) alternative is greater than one, choose the higher first cost alternative Ⓑ

EXAMPLE 10-3

Determine which alternative should be chosen based on a benefit/cost ratio, and a nominal interest rate of 7%. **Solution**: Use a benefit/cost ratio based on a Present Worth analysis. Note interest table numbers were used instead of formulas.

	A	B	B-A
initial cost	6000	9000	3000
Annual benefit	1000	1500	500
Salvage Value	1000	1800	800
life, years	10	10	

use Present Worth B/C

$$B/C_A = \frac{1000(P/A, 7\%, 10)}{6000 - 1000(P/F, 7\%, 10)} = \frac{1000(7.0236)}{6000 - 1000(0.5083)}$$

$$= \frac{7023.60}{5491.70} = \underline{1.28} \checkmark \text{ o.k.}$$

$$B/C_B = \frac{1500(P/A, 7\%, 10)}{9000 - 1800(P/F, 7\%, 10)} = \frac{1500(7.0236)}{9000 - 1800(0.5083)}$$

$$= \frac{10,535.40}{8085.06} = \underline{1.30} \checkmark \text{ OK}$$

$$\frac{\Delta B}{\Delta C}(B\text{-}A) = \frac{500(P/A, 7\%, 10)}{3000 - 800(P/F, 7\%, 10)} = \frac{500(7.0236)}{3000 - 800(0.5083)}$$

$$= \frac{3511.80}{2593.36} = \underline{\underline{1.35}} \checkmark \text{ choose } (B)$$

or

$$\frac{\Delta B}{\Delta C} = \frac{10,535.40 - 7023.60}{8085.06 - 5491.70} = \underline{1.35} \checkmark (B)$$

↑ using present worth numbers

EXAMPLE 10-4

So you have a choice of two used dump trucks for your growing excavation business. Based on a benefit/cost ratio, which alternative should you choose? Assume i=6%. **Solution**: Use a benefit/cost ratio based on a uniform annual analysis. (Yes this is allowed!) Notice the lives of the alternatives are different but this doesn't matter in an annual analysis.

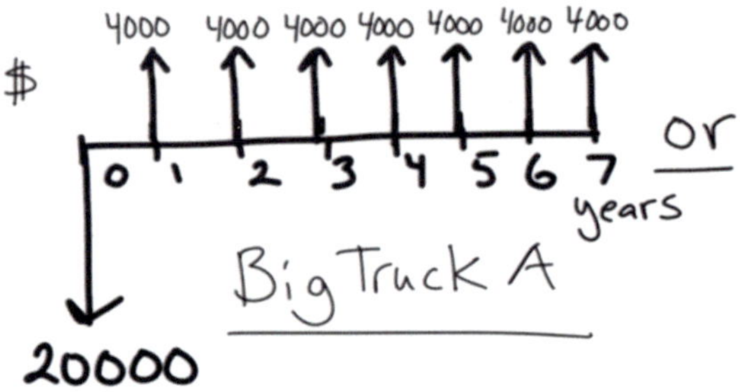

or

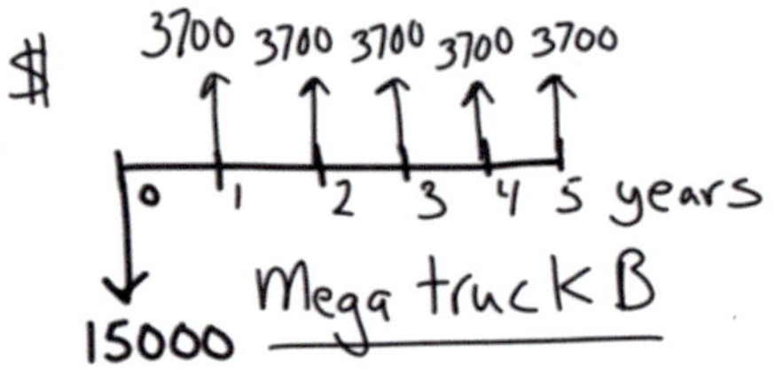

Ⓐ $\frac{B}{C} = \frac{4000}{P\left[\frac{i(1+i)^n}{(1+i)^n-1}\right]} = \frac{4000}{20{,}000\left[\frac{0.06(1+0.06)^7}{(1+0.06)^7-1}\right]} = \underline{\underline{1.17}}$ ✓ ok

$A=$ (denominator) $\leftarrow 3582$

Ⓑ $\frac{B}{C} = \frac{3700}{P\left[\frac{i(1+i)^n}{(1+i)^n-1}\right]} = \frac{3700}{15000\left[\frac{0.06(1+.06)^5}{(1+0.06)^5-1}\right]} = \underline{\underline{1.039}}$ ✓ ok

$A=$ (denominator) $\leftarrow 3560$

Incremental analysis

$\frac{\Delta B}{\Delta C} = \frac{4000-3700}{3582-3560} = \underline{\underline{13.6 \geq 1}}$ choose Big Truck Ⓐ

using annual analysis and given lives.

You can check this result picking a common denominator for the lifespans (35 years) with a repeating cashflow and determine the present worth of each alternative. You should get alternative A again.

EXAMPLE 10-5

Data for three mutually exclusive alternatives are given in the table below. For a MARR of 9%, determine the best alternative using benefit cost ratio analysis.

Alternative	Alt. A	Alt. B	Alt. C
Initial Cost	$7,000	$1,200	$1,800
Uniform Annual Benefits	$615	$350	$425
Useful life, years	20	5	10

Solution: Since the lives are different, use an Annual Benefit/Cost analysis assuming the alternatives repeat.

use $i = 9\%$ Check if all alternatives have a $B/C \geq 1$

Ⓐ $\frac{\text{Benefits}}{\text{Costs}} = \frac{615}{A = P\left[\frac{i(1+i)^n}{(1+i)^n - 1}\right]} = \frac{615}{7000\left[\frac{0.09(1+0.09)^{20}}{(1+0.09)^{20} - 1}\right]} = \frac{615}{766.82} = 0.8 < 1$ N.G.

Ⓑ $\frac{B}{C} = \frac{350}{1200\left[\frac{0.09(1+0.09)^5}{(1+0.09)^5 - 1}\right]} = \frac{350}{308.51} = 1.13 \geq 1$ ✓

Ⓒ $\frac{B}{C} = \frac{425}{1800\left[\frac{0.09(1+0.09)^{10}}{(1+0.09)^{10} - 1}\right]} = \frac{425}{280.476} = 1.52 \geq 1$ ✓

Incremental analysis to find "best" between B & C

(C−B) $\frac{B}{C} = \frac{425 - 350}{280.5 - 308.5} = -2.67 < 1$

(Pick B)

★ actually Ⓒ is better, see the graph on the next page

Example 10-4, Excel Solution – using a <u>Net Present Worth analysis</u>, you can see which alternative gives you the best present worth at different interest rates. At 9%, alternative C gives the most return for your money.

year	Alt. A	Alt. B	Alt. C	i	NPW A	NPW B	NPW C
0	-7000	-1200	-1800	0%	$5,300	$2,200	$4,900
1	615	350	425	1%	$4,098	$1,854	$4,240
2	615	350	425	2%	$3,056	$1,560	$3,673
3	615	350	425	3%	$2,150	$1,309	$3,184
4	615	350	425	4%	$1,358	$1,093	$2,760
5	615	-850	425	5%	$664	$908	$2,391
6	615	350	425	6%	$54	$747	$2,070
7	615	350	425	7%	($485)	$607	$1,787
8	615	350	425	8%	($962)	$486	$1,539
9	615	350	425	9%	($1,386)	$379	$1,319
10	615	-850	-1375	10%	($1,764)	$285	$1,124
11	615	350	425	11%	($2,103)	$202	$950
12	615	350	425	12%	($2,406)	$128	$795
13	615	350	425	13%	($2,680)	$62	$655
14	615	350	425	14%	($2,927)	$3	$529
15	615	-850	425	15%	($3,151)	($50)	$415
16	615	350	425	16%	($3,354)	($98)	$312
17	615	350	425	17%	($3,539)	($141)	$217
18	615	350	425	18%	($3,708)	($181)	$131
19	615	350	425	19%	($3,863)	($217)	$52
20	615	350	425	20%	($4,005)	($250)	($21)

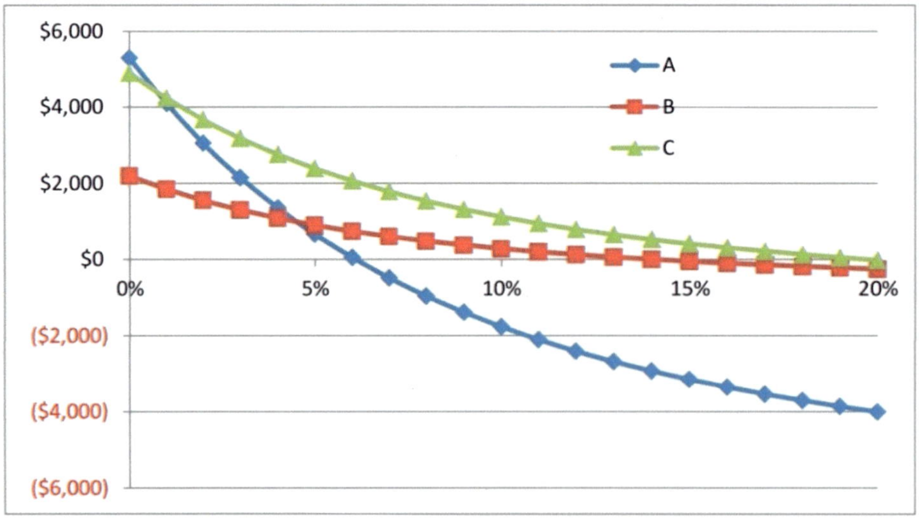

Use a 10 year life for B + C and a PW analysis $i = 9\%$

year	B	C	C−B
0	−1200	−1800	−600
1	350	425	75
2	350	425	75
3	350	425	75
4	350	425	75
5	−850	425	1275
6	350	425	75
7	350	425	75
8	350	425	75
9	350	425	75
10	350	425	75

$$PW_{C-B} \quad \Delta B/\Delta C = \frac{75(P/A, 9\%, 10) + 1200(P/F, 9\%, 5)}{600}$$

$$= \frac{75(6.418) + 1200(.6499)}{600} = \underline{2.1}$$

2.1 > 1 choose (C)

EXAMPLE 10-6

Given the cash flows in the table below for two different alternatives, determine which alternative should be selected, if any, if the interest rate is 5%, using a Present Worth Benefit - Cost (B/C) analysis.

	Cash Flow, $	
Year	Alt. A	Alt. B
0	-5000	-9000
1	2750	1000
2	2750	3000
3	2750	5000
4	2750	7000
5	4250	9000

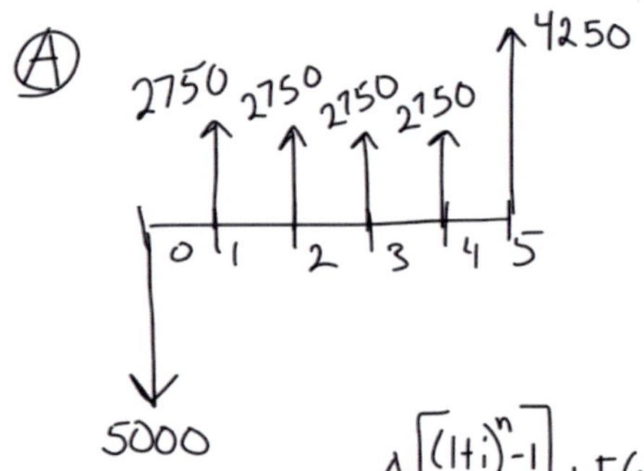

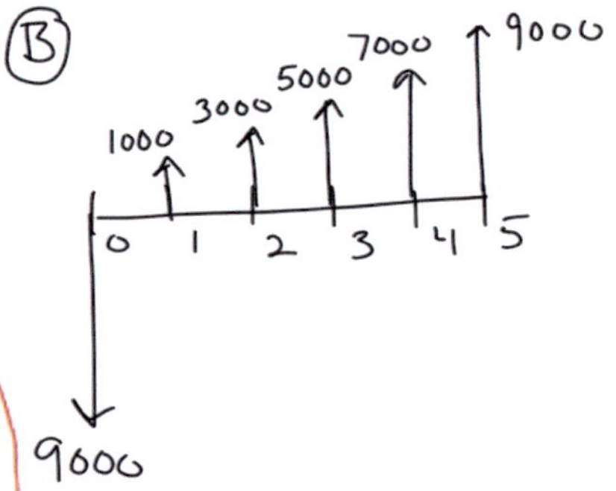

A

$$\frac{B}{C} = \frac{PW_{Ben}}{PW_{costs}} = \frac{A\left[\frac{(1+i)^n-1}{i(1+i)^n}\right] + F(1+i)^{-n}}{5000}$$

$$\frac{B}{C} = \frac{2750\left[\frac{(1+0.05)^5-1}{0.05(1+0.05)^5}\right] + 1500(1+0.05)^{-5}}{5000}$$

$$\frac{B}{C} = \frac{13081.35}{5000} = \underline{\underline{2.62}}$$

B

$$\frac{B}{C} = \frac{PW_{Ben}}{PW_{costs}}$$

$$\frac{B}{C} = \frac{A\left[\frac{(1+i)^n-1}{i(1+i)^n}\right] + G\left[\frac{(1+i)^n-in-1}{i^2(1+i)^n}\right]}{9000}$$

$$\frac{B}{C} = \frac{1000\left[\frac{(1+0.05)^5-1}{0.05(1+0.05)^5}\right] + 2000\left[\frac{(1+0.05)^5-0.05(5)-1}{0.05^2(1+0.05)^5}\right]}{9000}$$

Example 10-5 cont

Ⓑ $\frac{B}{C} = \frac{20803.31}{9000} = 2.31$

Require an incremental B/C analysis to choose "Best" alternative

Take B-A (higher first cost - lower first cost)

Ⓑ-Ⓐ CFD

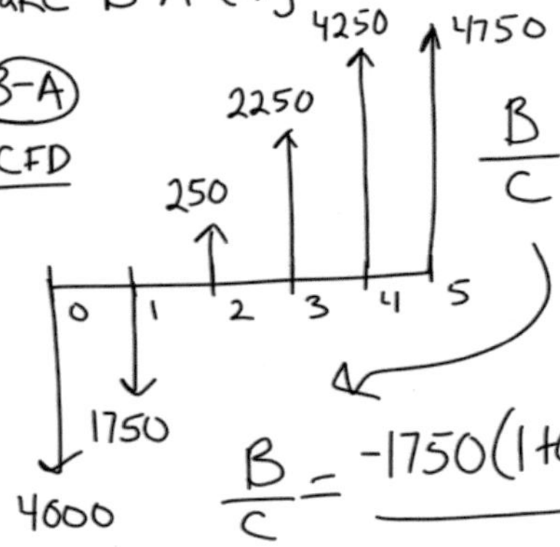

$$\frac{B}{C} = \frac{PW_{Ben}}{PW_{cost}} = \frac{F(1+i)^{-n} + F(1+i)^{-n} + F(1+i)^{-n} + F(1+i)^{-n} + F(1+i)^{-n}}{cost}$$

$$\frac{B}{C} = \frac{-1750(1+0.05)^{-1} + 250(1+0.05)^{-2} + 2250(1+0.05)^{-3} + 4250(1+0.05)^{-4} + 4750(1+0.05)^{-5}}{4000}$$

$$\frac{B}{C} = \frac{7,721.96}{4000} = 1.93 > 1 \Rightarrow \text{Since } \Delta B/\Delta C > 1$$ Ⓑ ✓

Choose higher first cost alternative

EXAMPLE 11-1

Determine the present worth of the cash flow given below, assuming a monthly interest rate of 1.25%.

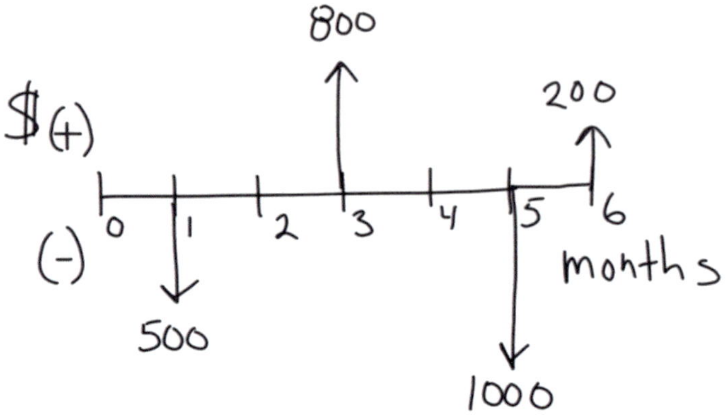

$$P = F(1+i)^{-n}$$

$$P = -500(1+0.0125)^{-1} + 800(1+0.0125)^{-3} + -1000(1+0.0125)^{-5} + 200(1+0.0125)^{-6}$$

$$P = \underline{\underline{-477.23}}$$

"Anyone who has never made a mistake has never tried anything new."

— Albert Einstein

EXAMPLE 11-2

Draw the cash flow diagram and determine the present worth of the cash flow given below, with an annual interest rate of 8%.

Year	0	1	2	3	4	5	6	7	8
Cash Flow	-P	1,000	1,150	1,300	1,450	1,600	1,600	1,600	1,600

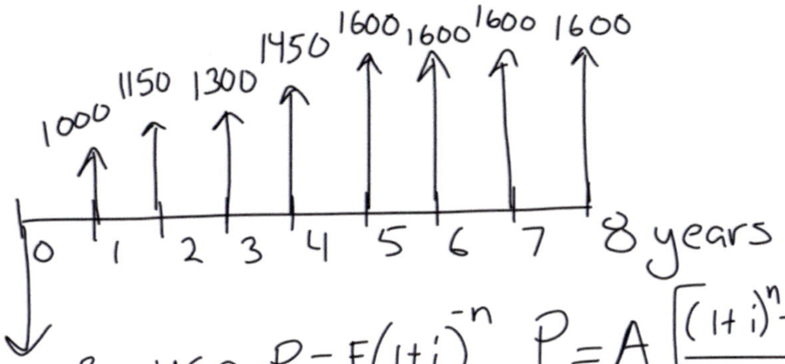

$P = ?$ use $P = F(1+i)^{-n}$ $\quad P = A\left[\frac{(1+i)^n - 1}{i(1+i)^n}\right]$ $\quad P = G\left[\frac{(1+i)^n - in - 1}{i^2(1+i)^n}\right]$

$$P = 1000\left[\frac{(1+0.08)^4 - 1}{0.08(1+0.08)^4}\right] + 150\left[\frac{(1+0.08)^4 - 0.08(4) - 1}{0.08^2(1+0.08)^4}\right]$$

$$+ 1600\left[\frac{(1+0.08)^4 - 1}{0.08(1+0.08)^4}\right](1+0.08)^{-4} = \$7904.86$$

Note: I moved the four payments of $1600 to year four, then moved that sum back to year zero. The first half of the cash flow (year zero to four) used an annual payment and a gradient.

"Have no fear of perfection - you'll never reach it."

— Salvador Dalí

EXAMPLE 11-3

Megastar engineering is considering a concrete finishing robot that will cost $20,000 to buy. After 7 years its salvage value will be $2000. An overhaul costing $5000 will be needed in Year 4. O&M costs will be $2500 per year. Profit will be $6000 per year.

Draw the cash flow diagram and find the rate of return for the cash flow.

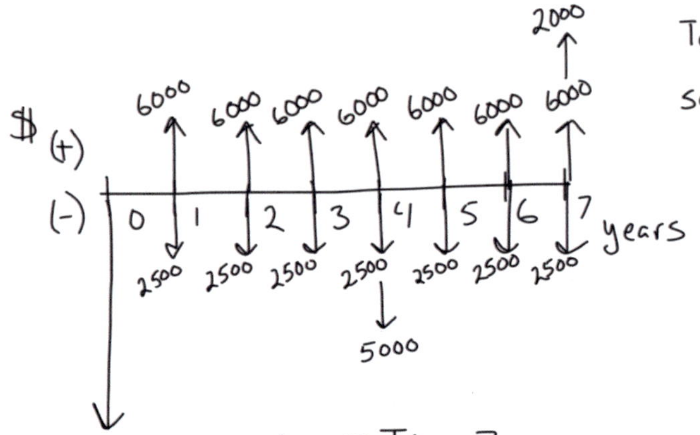

To find Rate of Return, IRR set Benefits = Costs solve for i (IRR)

Benefits = costs @ Time Zero

$$P = A\left[\frac{(1+i)^n-1}{i(1+i)^n}\right] + P = F(1+i)^n = P = A\left[\frac{(1+i)^n-1}{i(1+i)^n}\right] + P = F(1+i)^{-n} + \text{First Cost}$$

$$6000\left[\frac{(1+i)^7-1}{i(1+i)^7}\right] + 2000(1+i)^{-7} = 2500\left[\frac{(1+i)^7-1}{i(1+i)^7}\right] + 5000(1+i)^{-4} + 20{,}000$$

using a calculator solver or Excel or trial & error $i = IRR = 0.0172 \Rightarrow \underline{1.72\%}$

Not a great return on the money spent.

EXAMPLE 11-4

Data for two mutually exclusive alternatives (A and B) are given below:

Cash Flows	Alternative	
	A	B
Initial Cost	$3000	$2000
Annual Benefits (beginning at end of year 1)	$1000	$800
Annual Costs (beginning at end of year 1)	$300	$150
Salvage Value (Benefit)	$500	$0
Useful Life (years)	5	10

a) Draw the cash flow diagrams for the two alternatives based on a net present worth analysis (NPW).
b) Determine which alternative to select based on a net present worth (NPW) cash flow analysis, and a MARR = 7% interest rate.

Solution next page.

"We learn from failure, not from success!"
— Bram Stoker, Dracula

11-4 Solution: The convention, when you have unequal lives and want a present worth comparison, is to use a common denominator for the usable lifespan. In this case, use 10 years for both alternatives and assume alternative A repeats with exactly the same benefits and cost.

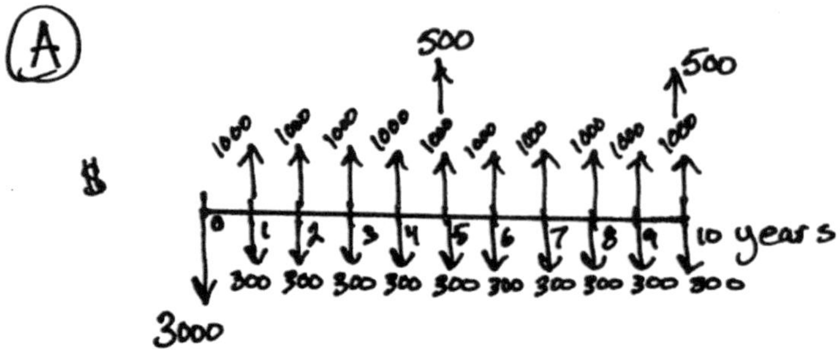

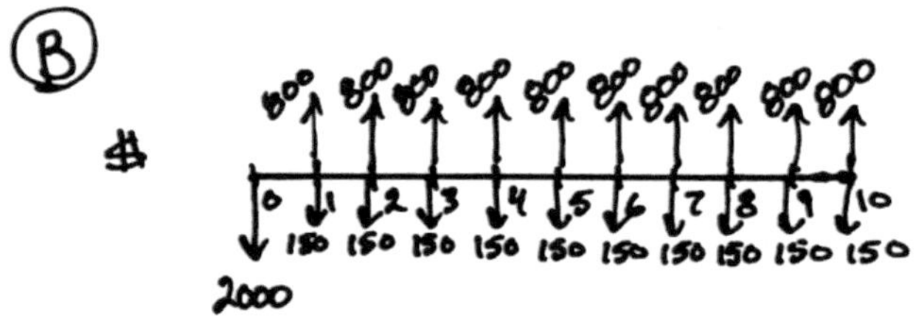

$$PW = \text{First cost} + A\left[\frac{(1+i)^n - 1}{i(1+i)^n}\right] + F(1+i)^{-n}$$

(A)

$$PW = -3000 + (1000-300)\left[\frac{(1+0.07)^{10}-1}{0.07(1+.07)^{10}}\right] + 500(1+0.07)^{-5} + 500(1+0.07)^{-10}$$

$$= \$2527.17$$

(B)

$$PW = -2000 + (800-150)\left[\frac{(1+.07)^{10}-1}{.07(1+0.07)^{10}}\right] = \$2565.33$$

Choose (B)

EXAMPLE 11-5

Data for two mutually exclusive alternatives (A and B) are given below:

Cash Flows	Alternative	
	A	B
Initial Cost	$3000	$2000
Annual Benefits (beginning at end of year 1)	$1000	$800
Annual Costs (beginning at end of year 1)	$300	$150
Salvage Value (Benefit)	$500	$0
Useful Life (years)	5	10

a) Draw the cash flow diagrams for the two alternatives based on an annual worth analysis.
b) Determine which alternative to select based on an annual cash flow analysis, and a MARR = 7% interest rate.

Solution next page.

"It takes guts and humility to admit mistakes. Admitting we're wrong is courage, not weakness."
— Roy T. Bennett, The Light in the Heart

11-5 cont.

Solution: This is example 8-4 solved in a different way. In this case the lives do not have to match because we assume the cash flow will repeat and we can just solve for an annual worth for each alternative and compare.

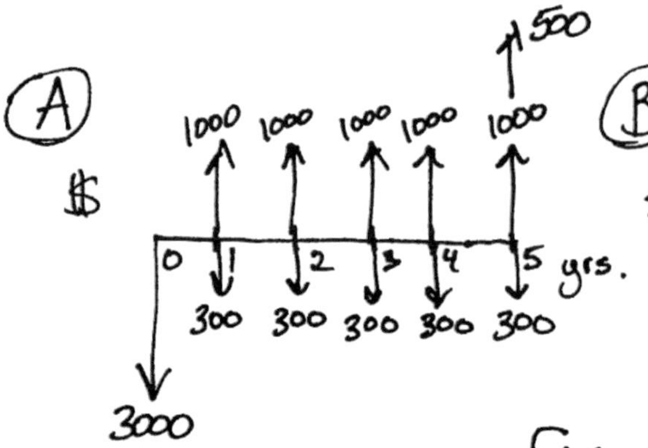

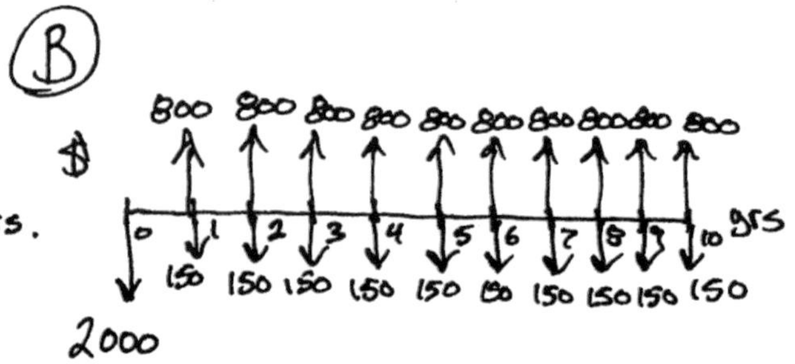

using $A = P\left[\frac{i(1+i)^n}{(1+i)^n - 1}\right]$ $A = F\left[\frac{i}{(1+i)^n - 1}\right]$

(A) $AW = (1000 - 300) - 3000\left[\frac{0.07(1+0.07)^5}{(1+0.07)^5 - 1}\right]$

$+ 500\left[\frac{.07}{(1+.07)^5 - 1}\right] = \$55.27$

(B) $AW = (800 - 150) - 2000\left[\frac{.07(1+.07)^{10}}{(1+.07)^{10} - 1}\right]$

$= \$365.24$ Pick B

EXAMPLE 11-6

The cash flows have a present value of 0. Compute the value of D, assuming a 9% interest rate.

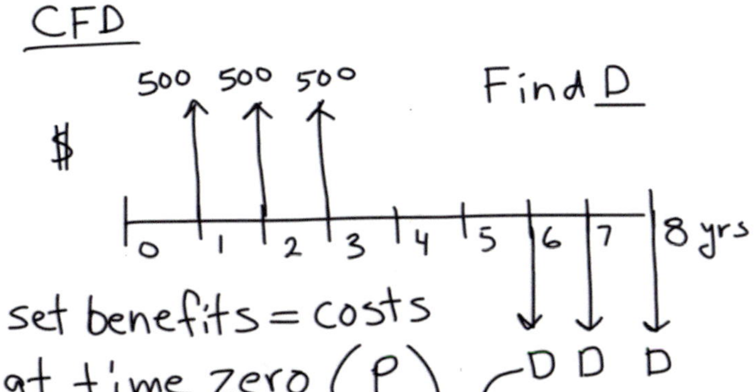

set benefits = costs at time zero (P_0)

moving D to P_5 then to P_0

$$P = A\left[\frac{(1+i)^n - 1}{i(1+i)^n}\right] = P_5 = A\left[\frac{(1+i)^n - 1}{i(1+i)^n}\right] \times P_0 = F(1+i)^{-n}$$

$$500\left[\frac{(1+0.09)^3 - 1}{0.09(1+0.09)^3}\right] = D\left[\frac{(1+0.09)^3 - 1}{0.09(1+0.09)^3}\right](1+0.09)^{-5}$$

$$\frac{1265.647}{(0.64993)(2.53129)} = D = \$769.31$$

"The 50-50-90 rule: anytime you have a 50-50 chance of getting something right, there's a 90% probability you'll get it wrong."

— Andy Rooney

EXAMPLE 11-7

What is the present worth of the following Cash flow Diagram at 6% interest rate?

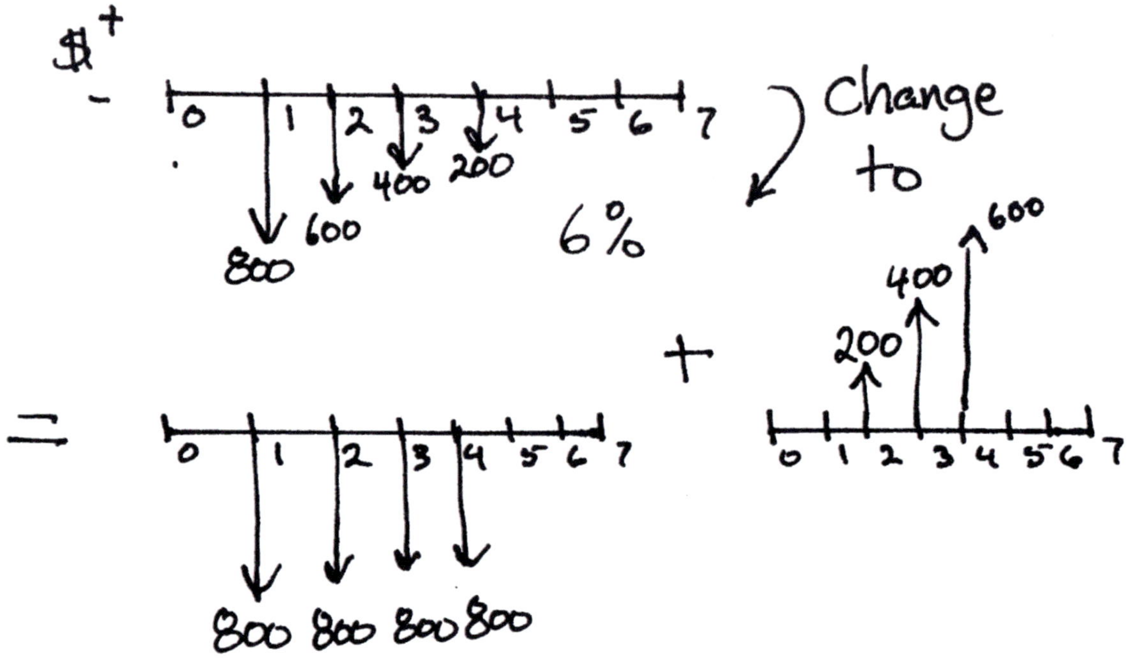

$$PW = -800\underbrace{\left[\frac{(1+.06)^4 - 1}{.06(1+0.06)^4}\right]}_{A} + 200\underbrace{\left[\frac{(1+.06)^4 - .06(4) - 1}{.06^2(1+.06)^4}\right]}_{G}$$

$$PW = \underline{-1782.98}$$

EXAMPLE 11-8

A contractor is looking at two alternatives for a bobcat. Assuming the alternatives are replaced at the end of their useful life, determine the better alternative using annual cash flow analysis at an interest rate of 4%.

Data	A	B
First Cost	$4,000	$6,000
Annual Cost	$1,000	$500
Annual Benefit	$2,000	$2,200
Life, Years	4	10
Salvage Value	$3,000	$1,000

(Solution next page)

Solution 11-8: When you have different alternatives with different lives, the assumption is made that the cash flows will repeat. So one way to do the problem is to have a common life, say 40 years, with alternative A repeat ten times and alternative B repeating four times and then calculate a present worth to see which alternative is better. The trick to making this problem easier to solve is recognizing that the cash flows will repeat (without changing) and using an annual cash flow analysis which doesn't require the lives to be the same.

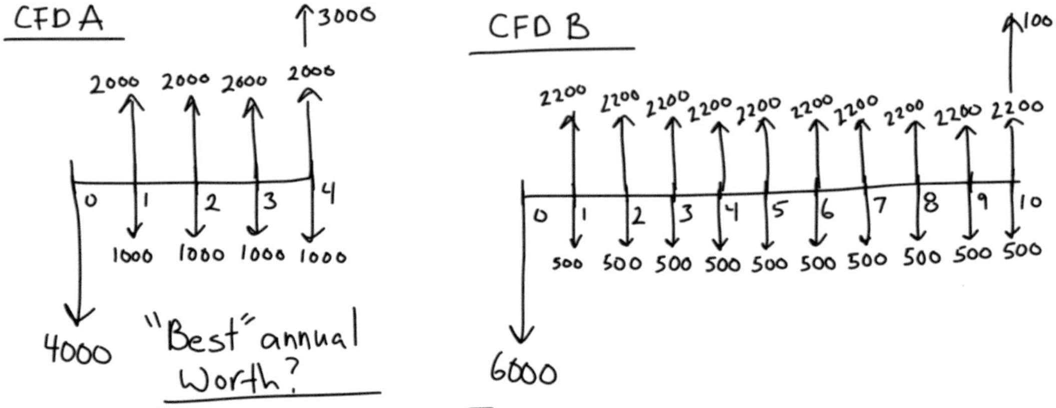

$$A_A = P\left[\frac{i(1+i)^n}{(1+i)^n - 1}\right] + 2000 - 1000 + F\left[\frac{i}{(1+i)^n - 1}\right]$$

$$= -4000\left[\frac{0.04(1+0.04)^4}{(1+0.04)^4 - 1}\right] + 2000 - 1000 + 3000\left[\frac{0.04}{(1+0.04)^4 - 1}\right] = \$604{,}51 \text{ / per year}$$

$$A_B = -6000\left[\frac{0.04(1+0.04)^{10}}{(1+0.04)^{10} - 1}\right] + 2200 - 500 + 1000\left[\frac{0.04}{(1+0.04)^{10} - 1}\right] = \$1043{,}55 \text{ / per year}$$

Choose (B) ✓

EXAMPLE 11-9

The cash flows for two different alternatives are given in table below.

Data	Alternative		
	X	Y	Y-X
Initial Cost	$8,000	$30,000	$22,000
Net Benefits / year	$1,225	$3,120	$1,895
Salvage	0	$2400	$2,400
Life, Year	20	20	20
ROR	14%	8.5%	

Each alternative has a 20-year useful life with no salvage value. If the MARR is set at 7%, determine which is the best alternative, using an incremental rate of return analysis (IRR)?

Solution 11-9: Calculate an incremental analysis, since you were given the rate of return for each alternative, and both alternatives have a better IRR than the MARR. Choose which is better at the MARR.

year	Y−X
0	-22,000
1	1895
2	1895
3	1895
4	1895
5	1895
⋮	⋮
19	1895
20	4295

set Benefits = costs Solve for i (ΔIRR

$$P = A\left[\frac{(1+i)^n - 1}{i(1+i)^n}\right] + P = F(1+i)^{-n} = 22{,}000$$

(S.V.)

$$1895\left[\frac{(1+i)^{20} - 1}{i(1+i)^{20}}\right] + 2400(1+i)^{-20} = 22{,}000$$

$$i = \Delta IRR = 0.06258 = 6.3\% < 7\%$$

* Incremental Analysis
higher first cost − lower first cost
if ΔIRR > MARR choose higher
if ΔIRR < MARR choose lower

Choose (X)

See how this problem looks in graph form on the next page. You can see on the graph, at 7%, alternative X gives you the better Present Worth.

Example 11-9 Using Excel

At 7%, alternative X is the better choice. Look at the Choice Table in the graph below.

year	X	Y	Y-X	Interst rate	PW X	PW Y
0	-8000	-30000	-22000	0	$16,500.00	$34,800.00
1	1225	3120	1895	2	$12,030.51	$22,631.60
2	1225	3120	1895	4	$8,648.15	$13,497.15
3	1225	3120	1895	6	$6,050.65	$6,534.49
4	1225	3120	1895	8	$4,027.23	$1,147.54
5	1225	3120	1895	10	$2,429.12	($3,080.94)
6	1225	3120	1895	12	$1,150.07	($6,446.54)
7	1225	3120	1895	14	$113.33	($9,161.20)
8	1225	3120	1895	16	($737.17)	($11,378.69)
9	1225	3120	1895	18	($1,442.89)	($13,211.82)
10	1225	3120	1895	20	($2,034.76)	($14,744.31)
11	1225	3120	1895	22	($2,536.17)	($16,038.99)
12	1225	3120	1895	24	($2,964.94)	($17,143.51)
13	1225	3120	1895	26	($3,334.78)	($18,094.38)
14	1225	3120	1895	28	($3,656.39)	($18,919.87)
15	1225	3120	1895	30	($3,938.15)	($19,642.09)
16	1225	3120	1895	32	($4,186.72)	($20,278.50)
17	1225	3120	1895	34	($4,407.40)	($20,842.98)
18	1225	3120	1895	36	($4,604.48)	($21,346.71)
19	1225	3120	1895	38	($4,781.45)	($21,798.73)
20	1225	5520	4295	40	($4,941.16)	($22,206.45)
irr =	14.2%	8.5%	6.3%			

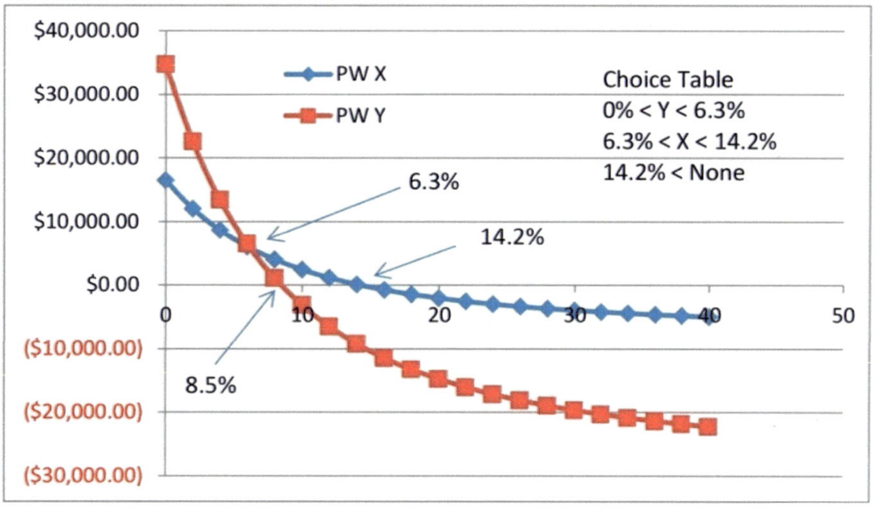

EXAMPLE 11-10

Given the cash flows in the table below for three different alternatives, determine which alternative should be selected using a **Future Worth analysis**, if the interest rate is 7%.

	Cash Flow, $		
Year	Alt. A	Alt. B	Alt. C
0	-4,750	-8200	-12,000
1	1,600	0	3,000
2	1,600	0	4,000
3	1,600	4500	5,000
4	1,800	7000	6,000

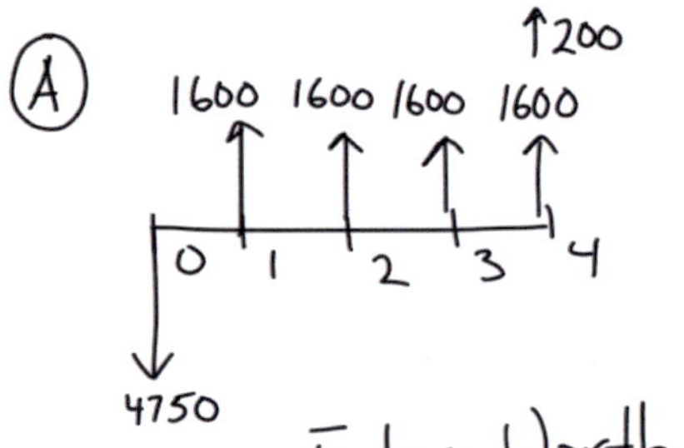

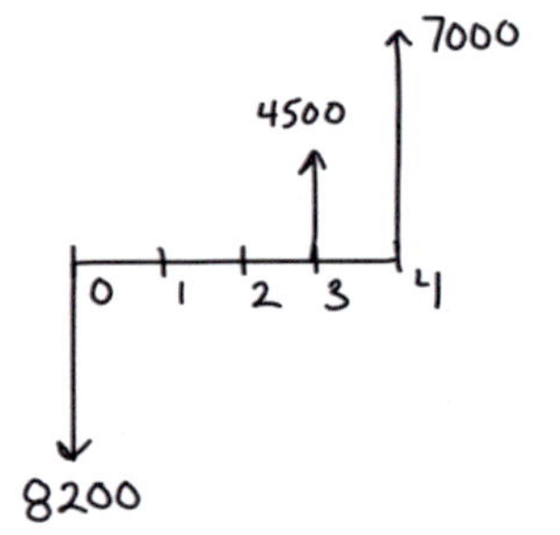

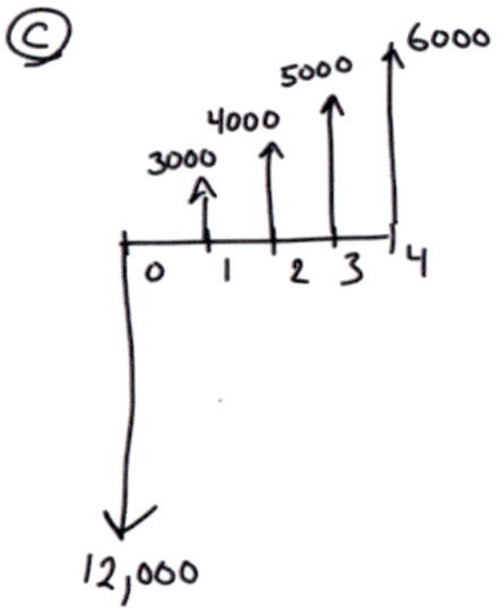

Future Worth

(A) $FW = F = P(1+i)^n + F = A\left[\frac{(1+i)^n - 1}{i}\right] + 200$

$FW_A = -4750(1+0.07)^4 + 1600\left[\frac{(1+0.07)^4 - 1}{.07}\right] + 200 = \$1077.63$

(B) $FW_B = -8200(1+0.07)^4 + 4500(1+0.07)^1 + 7000 = \$1066.47$

(C) $FW_C = -12000(1+0.07)^4 + 3000\left[\frac{(1+0.07)^4 - 1}{0.07}\right] + 1000\left[\frac{(1+0.07)^4 - 0.07(4) - 1}{0.07^2(1+0.07)^4}\right](1+0.07)^4$

(A above the 3000 term; G above the 1000 term; "move to P_0" and "move to F_4" noted above the gradient bracket and the $(1+0.07)^4$ factor)

$= 3875.18$

Choose C →

EXAMPLE 11-11

You want to buy a bulldozer and can pay a \$40,000 down payment and a payment of \$1,200 each month. Ten year monthly loans are available for **8% per year**. What is the most expensive bulldozer you can buy?

Down Payment = \$40,000

$n = 10(12) = 120$ months

$A = \$1200$

$$i/\text{month} = \frac{8\%}{12} = 0.667\%$$

$$A = P\left[\frac{i(1+i)^n}{(1+i)^n - 1}\right]$$

$$1200 = (P - 40{,}000)\left[\frac{0.0067(1+0.0067)^{120}}{(1+0.0067)^{120} - 1}\right]$$

$$P = \$138{,}733.69$$

EXAMPLE 11-12

You want to buy a house for \$200,000 with a 20% down payment.
The interest rate is 6%, compounded monthly.

1) How much will be your monthly payment?

2) How much interest will be paid on the loan? $i = \frac{.06}{12} = .005/\text{month}$

① $$A = P\left[\frac{i(1+i)^n}{(1+i)^n - 1}\right] = \$160{,}000\left[\frac{.005(1+.005)^{360}}{(1+.005)^{360} - 1}\right]$$

$$= \$959.28/\text{month}$$

360 payments (in 30 yrs)

② Total = \$959.28 × 360 = \$345,341.10

345,341 − 160,000 = \$185,341

interest on loan

Wow!

EXAMPLE 11-13

If $i = 11\%$ for what value of A is the present value $= \phi$ (zero)

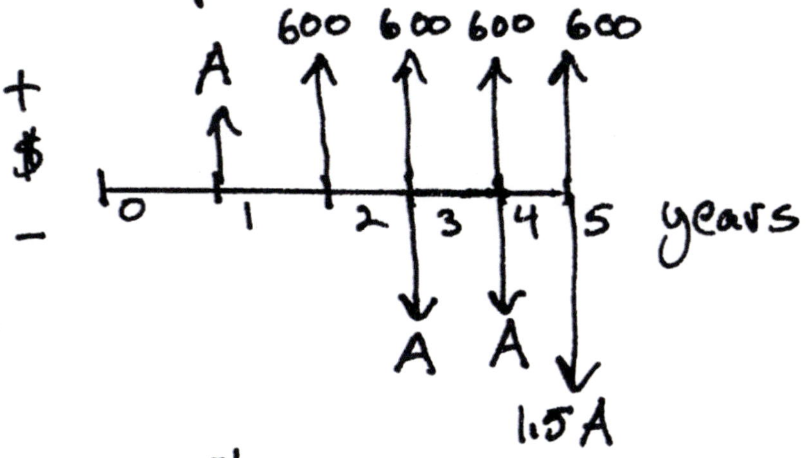

$$0 = A(1+.11)^{-1} + 600\left[\frac{(1+.11)^4-1}{.11(1+.11)^4}\right](1+.11)^{-1}$$

$$-A\left[\frac{(1+.11)^3-1}{.11(1+.11)^3}\right](1+.11)^{-2} - .5A(1+.11)^{-5}$$

Solve for $A = \$1215.94$

CHAPTER 12 – ENGINEERING ETHICS AND SUSTAINABILITY

When you think of the most trustworthy professionals, engineers will typically rank in the top five. One of the reasons for this is our teaching and following of an Engineering Ethics Code of Conduct. The code guides our decision making and helps us to deal with perilous ethical situations.

Top honest and ethical professions (Typical ranking):

1. Nurses
2. Pharmacists
2. Doctors
4. Engineers
5. School teachers

Now each country has a code of ethics for their engineering profession but I think the American Society of Engineering code of ethics (ASCE) gives a good overview of what is expected of engineers.

Fundamental Canons (courtesy ASCE www.asce.org/code_of_ethics/)

1. Engineers shall hold paramount the safety, health and welfare of the public and shall strive to comply with the principles of sustainable development in the performance of their professional duties.

Engineers often design facilities for the public, roads, bridges and buildings, and products, like car seats, rockets, and socks, where safety concerns are paramount. (Well maybe not socks, but they could be too tight and affect your circulation.) Problems creep in when engineers are asked to trim corners or look the other way because the cost to design a good product or fix a problem would be prohibitive.

The second part of the canon is sustainable development. This is a fairly new addition to the code and implies that an engineer should not only look at the micro implications of a project but the macro implications to the larger world. This is obviously very difficult to accomplish but acknowledging the goal and then trying to meet the goal, is a good first step.

2. Engineers shall perform services only in areas of their competence.

In the United States, getting a professional engineering license allows you to practice in any field of engineering. (In the states where you are registered) For example, you could be a structural engineer in the morning, a transportation engineer at lunch and a geotechnical engineer in the afternoon. You could sign plans for all three as long as you feel competent in each discipline *and* you can prove it if you are called into court over one of your decisions.

This freedom is great if you like to move between disciplines or the job market requires you to make a change but it does require an engineer to become "competent" in each discipline. What defines competent, well if you are unlucky and make some bad choices, the courts will decide. Better we take it upon ourselves to be a professional in our chosen field, so only work in areas in which you have the requisite skills.

3. Engineers shall issue public statements only in an objective and truthful manner.

I like to think this canon stops any engineer from becoming a politician. The intent of the canon is really the basis for our profession, if you can't believe what an engineer tells the public, how could you possibly trust any engineer.

You want an engineer telling the truth about your drinking water or how safe your automobile is in protecting your family. You want an engineer to make statements without political or business influences shading their comments. You want engineers to tell the truth, especially in public.

4. Engineers shall act in professional matters for each employer or client as faithful agents or trustees, and shall avoid conflicts of interest.

Engineers are required to act in good faith for their employer,

5. Engineers shall build their professional reputation on the merit of their services and shall not compete unfairly with others.

In the United States, engineering services are typically not a low bid commodity. An organization, such as a state department of transportation, will put out a request for engineering interest in a project. Say you want a bridge designed, engineering firms would send in their qualifications and be judged on their reputation. Then once a firm is picked for the job, the price, for the design services, is negotiated. This stops firms from getting into bidding wars. Engineering services should never be low bid.

6. Engineers shall act in such a manner as to uphold and enhance the honor, integrity, and dignity of the engineering profession and shall act with zero-tolerance for bribery, fraud, and corruption.

I think this speaks for itself.

7. Engineers shall continue their professional development throughout their careers, and shall provide opportunities for the professional development of those engineers under their supervision.

Engineers in most states are required to gain a set number of professional development hours (PDH) every two years to keep their licenses. I have to get 30 hours of PDHs every year to keep my P.E. license. (This book probably gives me 10 pdhs!)

To sum up, ethics are something that engineers should be aware of all the time. Someday, you will face a questionable situation and the more you know about ethics, the more case studies you read, the better prepared you will be to handle the problem. Don't go all whistleblower until it is a last resort…

COMPOUND INTEREST TABLES

Compound interest tables can be used to solve problems quickly. The tables below are developed for different i and n values so instead of using the formulas, a value can be selected based on the appropriate interest rate and number of periods.

Interest tables

ie)

$$P = F(1+i)^{-n} = F(P/F, i, n)$$

Want P knowing F

Interest rate

number of periods

$(1+i)^{-n}$ → developed into an Interest table

$$A = F\left[\frac{i}{(1+i)^n - 1}\right] = F(A/F, i, n)$$

$(A/F, i, n)$ → Interest table value

Want A knowing F

→ check A/F column knowing i and n

Compound Interest Factors

Interest Rate, i	$(1+i)^{-n}$	$(1+i)^{n}$	$\left[\frac{i(1+i)^n}{(1+i)^n-1}\right]$	$\left[\frac{i}{(1+i)^n-1}\right]$	$\left[\frac{(1+i)^n-1}{i(1+i)^n}\right]$	$\left[\frac{(1+i)^n-1}{i}\right]$	$\left[\frac{(1+i)^n-in-1}{i^2(1+i)^n}\right]$	$\left[\frac{(1+i)^n-in-1}{i(1+i)^n-i}\right]$	
1.00%	Find P	Find F	Find A	Find A	Find P	Find F	Find P	Find A	1.00%
	Know F	Know P	Know P	Know F	Know A	Know A	Know G	Know G	
n	P/F	F/P	A/P	A/F	P/A	F/A	P/G	A/G	n
1	0.9901	1.0100	1.0100	1.0000	0.9901	1.0000	0.0000	0.0000	1
2	0.9803	1.0201	0.5075	0.4975	1.9704	2.0100	0.9803	0.4975	2
3	0.9706	1.0303	0.3400	0.3300	2.9410	3.0301	2.9215	0.9934	3
4	0.9610	1.0406	0.2563	0.2463	3.9020	4.0604	5.8044	1.4876	4
5	0.9515	1.0510	0.2060	0.1960	4.8534	5.1010	9.6103	1.9801	5
6	0.9420	1.0615	0.1725	0.1625	5.7955	6.1520	14.3205	2.4710	6
7	0.9327	1.0721	0.1486	0.1386	6.7282	7.2135	19.9168	2.9602	7
8	0.9235	1.0829	0.1307	0.1207	7.6517	8.2857	26.3812	3.4478	8
9	0.9143	1.0937	0.1167	0.1067	8.5660	9.3685	33.6959	3.9337	9
10	0.9053	1.1046	0.1056	0.0956	9.4713	10.4622	41.8435	4.4179	10
11	0.8963	1.1157	0.0965	0.0865	10.3676	11.5668	50.8067	4.9005	11
12	0.8874	1.1268	0.0888	0.0788	11.2551	12.6825	60.5687	5.3815	12
13	0.8787	1.1381	0.0824	0.0724	12.1337	13.8093	71.1126	5.8607	13
14	0.8700	1.1495	0.0769	0.0669	13.0037	14.9474	82.4221	6.3384	14
15	0.8613	1.1610	0.0721	0.0621	13.8651	16.0969	94.4810	6.8143	15
16	0.8528	1.1726	0.0679	0.0579	14.7179	17.2579	107.2734	7.2886	16
17	0.8444	1.1843	0.0643	0.0543	15.5623	18.4304	120.7834	7.7613	17
18	0.8360	1.1961	0.0610	0.0510	16.3983	19.6147	134.9957	8.2323	18
19	0.8277	1.2081	0.0581	0.0481	17.2260	20.8109	149.8950	8.7017	19
20	0.8195	1.2202	0.0554	0.0454	18.0456	22.0190	165.4664	9.1694	20
21	0.8114	1.2324	0.0530	0.0430	18.8570	23.2392	181.6950	9.6354	21
22	0.8034	1.2447	0.0509	0.0409	19.6604	24.4716	198.5663	10.0998	22
23	0.7954	1.2572	0.0489	0.0389	20.4558	25.7163	216.0660	10.5626	23
24	0.7876	1.2697	0.0471	0.0371	21.2434	26.9735	234.1800	11.0237	24
25	0.7798	1.2824	0.0454	0.0354	22.0232	28.2432	252.8945	11.4831	25
26	0.7720	1.2953	0.0439	0.0339	22.7952	29.5256	272.1957	11.9409	26
27	0.7644	1.3082	0.0424	0.0324	23.5596	30.8209	292.0702	12.3971	27
28	0.7568	1.3213	0.0411	0.0311	24.3164	32.1291	312.5047	12.8516	28
29	0.7493	1.3345	0.0399	0.0299	25.0658	33.4504	333.4863	13.3044	29
30	0.7419	1.3478	0.0387	0.0287	25.8077	34.7849	355.0021	13.7557	30
40	0.6717	1.4889	0.0305	0.0205	32.8347	48.8864	596.8561	18.1776	40
45	0.6391	1.5648	0.0277	0.0177	36.0945	56.4811	733.7037	20.3273	45
50	0.6080	1.6446	0.0255	0.0155	39.1961	64.4632	879.4176	22.4363	50
55	0.5785	1.7285	0.0237	0.0137	42.1472	72.8525	1032.8148	24.5049	55
60	0.5504	1.8167	0.0222	0.0122	44.9550	81.6697	1192.8061	26.5333	60
65	0.5237	1.9094	0.0210	0.0110	47.6266	90.9366	1358.3903	28.5217	65
70	0.4983	2.0068	0.0199	0.0099	50.1685	100.6763	1528.6474	30.4703	70
75	0.4741	2.1091	0.0190	0.0090	52.5871	110.9128	1702.7340	32.3793	75
80	0.4511	2.2167	0.0182	0.0082	54.8882	121.6715	1879.8771	34.2492	80
85	0.4292	2.3298	0.0175	0.0075	57.0777	132.9790	2059.3701	36.0801	85
90	0.4084	2.4486	0.0169	0.0069	59.1609	144.8633	2240.5675	37.8724	90
95	0.3886	2.5735	0.0164	0.0064	61.1430	157.3538	2422.8811	39.6265	95
100	0.3697	2.7048	0.0159	0.0059	63.0289	170.4814	2605.7758	41.3426	100

Compound Interest Factors

Interest Rate, i	$(1+i)^{-n}$	$(1+i)^{n}$	$\left[\frac{i(1+i)^n}{(1+i)^n-1}\right]$	$\left[\frac{i}{(1+i)^n-1}\right]$	$\left[\frac{(1+i)^n-1}{i(1+i)^n}\right]$	$\left[\frac{(1+i)^n-1}{i}\right]$	$\left[\frac{(1+i)^n-in-1}{i^2(1+i)^n}\right]$	$\left[\frac{(1+i)^n-in-1}{i(1+i)^n-i}\right]$	
2.00%	Find P	Find F	Find A	Find A	Find P	Find F	Find P	Find A	2.00%
	Know F	Know P	Know P	Know F	Know A	Know A	Know G	Know G	
n	P/F	F/P	A/P	A/F	P/A	F/A	P/G	A/G	n
1	0.9804	1.0200	1.0200	1.0000	0.9804	1.0000	0.0000	0.0000	1
2	0.9612	1.0404	0.5150	0.4950	1.9416	2.0200	0.9612	0.4950	2
3	0.9423	1.0612	0.3468	0.3268	2.8839	3.0604	2.8458	0.9868	3
4	0.9238	1.0824	0.2626	0.2426	3.8077	4.1216	5.6173	1.4752	4
5	0.9057	1.1041	0.2122	0.1922	4.7135	5.2040	9.2403	1.9604	5
6	0.8880	1.1262	0.1785	0.1585	5.6014	6.3081	13.6801	2.4423	6
7	0.8706	1.1487	0.1545	0.1345	6.4720	7.4343	18.9035	2.9208	7
8	0.8535	1.1717	0.1365	0.1165	7.3255	8.5830	24.8779	3.3961	8
9	0.8368	1.1951	0.1225	0.1025	8.1622	9.7546	31.5720	3.8681	9
10	0.8203	1.2190	0.1113	0.0913	8.9826	10.9497	38.9551	4.3367	10
11	0.8043	1.2434	0.1022	0.0822	9.7868	12.1687	46.9977	4.8021	11
12	0.7885	1.2682	0.0946	0.0746	10.5753	13.4121	55.6712	5.2642	12
13	0.7730	1.2936	0.0881	0.0681	11.3484	14.6803	64.9475	5.7231	13
14	0.7579	1.3195	0.0826	0.0626	12.1062	15.9739	74.7999	6.1786	14
15	0.7430	1.3459	0.0778	0.0578	12.8493	17.2934	85.2021	6.6309	15
16	0.7284	1.3728	0.0737	0.0537	13.5777	18.6393	96.1288	7.0799	16
17	0.7142	1.4002	0.0700	0.0500	14.2919	20.0121	107.5554	7.5256	17
18	0.7002	1.4282	0.0667	0.0467	14.9920	21.4123	119.4581	7.9681	18
19	0.6864	1.4568	0.0638	0.0438	15.6785	22.8406	131.8139	8.4073	19
20	0.6730	1.4859	0.0612	0.0412	16.3514	24.2974	144.6003	8.8433	20
21	0.6598	1.5157	0.0588	0.0388	17.0112	25.7833	157.7959	9.2760	21
22	0.6468	1.5460	0.0566	0.0366	17.6580	27.2990	171.3795	9.7055	22
23	0.6342	1.5769	0.0547	0.0347	18.2922	28.8450	185.3309	10.1317	23
24	0.6217	1.6084	0.0529	0.0329	18.9139	30.4219	199.6305	10.5547	24
25	0.6095	1.6406	0.0512	0.0312	19.5235	32.0303	214.2592	10.9745	25
26	0.5976	1.6734	0.0497	0.0297	20.1210	33.6709	229.1987	11.3910	26
27	0.5859	1.7069	0.0483	0.0283	20.7069	35.3443	244.4311	11.8043	27
28	0.5744	1.7410	0.0470	0.0270	21.2813	37.0512	259.9392	12.2145	28
29	0.5631	1.7758	0.0458	0.0258	21.8444	38.7922	275.7064	12.6214	29
30	0.5521	1.8114	0.0446	0.0246	22.3965	40.5681	291.7164	13.0251	30
40	0.4529	2.2080	0.0366	0.0166	27.3555	60.4020	461.9931	16.8885	40
45	0.4102	2.4379	0.0339	0.0139	29.4902	71.8927	551.5652	18.7034	45
50	0.3715	2.6916	0.0318	0.0118	31.4236	84.5794	642.3606	20.4420	50
55	0.3365	2.9717	0.0301	0.0101	33.1748	98.5865	733.3527	22.1057	55
60	0.3048	3.2810	0.0288	0.0088	34.7609	114.0515	823.6975	23.6961	60
65	0.2761	3.6225	0.0276	0.0076	36.1975	131.1262	912.7085	25.2147	65
70	0.2500	3.9996	0.0267	0.0067	37.4986	149.9779	999.8343	26.6632	70
75	0.2265	4.4158	0.0259	0.0059	38.6771	170.7918	1084.6393	28.0434	75
80	0.2051	4.8754	0.0252	0.0052	39.7445	193.7720	1166.7868	29.3572	80
85	0.1858	5.3829	0.0246	0.0046	40.7113	219.1439	1246.0241	30.6064	85
90	0.1683	5.9431	0.0240	0.0040	41.5869	247.1567	1322.1701	31.7929	90
95	0.1524	6.5617	0.0236	0.0036	42.3800	278.0850	1395.1033	32.9189	95
100	0.1380	7.2446	0.0232	0.0032	43.0984	312.2323	1464.7527	33.9863	100

Compound Interest Factors

Interest Rate, i	$(1+i)^{-n}$	$(1+i)^{n}$	$\left[\frac{i(1+i)^n}{(1+i)^n-1}\right]$	$\left[\frac{i}{(1+i)^n-1}\right]$	$\left[\frac{(1+i)^n-1}{i(1+i)^n}\right]$	$\left[\frac{(1+i)^n-1}{i}\right]$	$\left[\frac{(1+i)^n-in-1}{i^2(1+i)^n}\right]$	$\left[\frac{(1+i)^n-in-1}{i(1+i)^n-i}\right]$	
3.00%	Find P	Find F	Find A	Find A	Find P	Find F	Find P	Find A	3.00%
	Know F	Know P	Know P	Know F	Know A	Know A	Know G	Know G	
n	P/F	F/P	A/P	A/F	P/A	F/A	P/G	A/G	n
1	0.9709	1.0300	1.0300	1.0000	0.9709	1.0000	0.0000	0.0000	1
2	0.9426	1.0609	0.5226	0.4926	1.9135	2.0300	0.9426	0.4926	2
3	0.9151	1.0927	0.3535	0.3235	2.8286	3.0909	2.7729	0.9803	3
4	0.8885	1.1255	0.2690	0.2390	3.7171	4.1836	5.4383	1.4631	4
5	0.8626	1.1593	0.2184	0.1884	4.5797	5.3091	8.8888	1.9409	5
6	0.8375	1.1941	0.1846	0.1546	5.4172	6.4684	13.0762	2.4138	6
7	0.8131	1.2299	0.1605	0.1305	6.2303	7.6625	17.9547	2.8819	7
8	0.7894	1.2668	0.1425	0.1125	7.0197	8.8923	23.4806	3.3450	8
9	0.7664	1.3048	0.1284	0.0984	7.7861	10.1591	29.6119	3.8032	9
10	0.7441	1.3439	0.1172	0.0872	8.5302	11.4639	36.3088	4.2565	10
11	0.7224	1.3842	0.1081	0.0781	9.2526	12.8078	43.5330	4.7049	11
12	0.7014	1.4258	0.1005	0.0705	9.9540	14.1920	51.2482	5.1485	12
13	0.6810	1.4685	0.0940	0.0640	10.6350	15.6178	59.4196	5.5872	13
14	0.6611	1.5126	0.0885	0.0585	11.2961	17.0863	68.0141	6.0210	14
15	0.6419	1.5580	0.0838	0.0538	11.9379	18.5989	77.0002	6.4500	15
16	0.6232	1.6047	0.0796	0.0496	12.5611	20.1569	86.3477	6.8742	16
17	0.6050	1.6528	0.0760	0.0460	13.1661	21.7616	96.0280	7.2936	17
18	0.5874	1.7024	0.0727	0.0427	13.7535	23.4144	106.0137	7.7081	18
19	0.5703	1.7535	0.0698	0.0398	14.3238	25.1169	116.2788	8.1179	19
20	0.5537	1.8061	0.0672	0.0372	14.8775	26.8704	126.7987	8.5229	20
21	0.5375	1.8603	0.0649	0.0349	15.4150	28.6765	137.5496	8.9231	21
22	0.5219	1.9161	0.0627	0.0327	15.9369	30.5368	148.5094	9.3186	22
23	0.5067	1.9736	0.0608	0.0308	16.4436	32.4529	159.6566	9.7093	23
24	0.4919	2.0328	0.0590	0.0290	16.9355	34.4265	170.9711	10.0954	24
25	0.4776	2.0938	0.0574	0.0274	17.4131	36.4593	182.4336	10.4768	25
26	0.4637	2.1566	0.0559	0.0259	17.8768	38.5530	194.0260	10.8535	26
27	0.4502	2.2213	0.0546	0.0246	18.3270	40.7096	205.7309	11.2255	27
28	0.4371	2.2879	0.0533	0.0233	18.7641	42.9309	217.5320	11.5930	28
29	0.4243	2.3566	0.0521	0.0221	19.1885	45.2189	229.4137	11.9558	29
30	0.4120	2.4273	0.0510	0.0210	19.6004	47.5754	241.3613	12.3141	30
40	0.3066	3.2620	0.0433	0.0133	23.1148	75.4013	361.7499	15.6502	40
45	0.2644	3.7816	0.0408	0.0108	24.5187	92.7199	420.6325	17.1556	45
50	0.2281	4.3839	0.0389	0.0089	25.7298	112.7969	477.4803	18.5575	50
55	0.1968	5.0821	0.0373	0.0073	26.7744	136.0716	531.7411	19.8600	55
60	0.1697	5.8916	0.0361	0.0061	27.6756	163.0534	583.0526	21.0674	60
65	0.1464	6.8300	0.0351	0.0051	28.4529	194.3328	631.2010	22.1841	65
70	0.1263	7.9178	0.0343	0.0043	29.1234	230.5941	676.0869	23.2145	70
75	0.1089	9.1789	0.0337	0.0037	29.7018	272.6309	717.6978	24.1634	75
80	0.0940	10.6409	0.0331	0.0031	30.2008	321.3630	756.0865	25.0353	80
85	0.0811	12.3357	0.0326	0.0026	30.6312	377.8570	791.3529	25.8349	85
90	0.0699	14.3005	0.0323	0.0023	31.0024	443.3489	823.6302	26.5667	90
95	0.0603	16.5782	0.0319	0.0019	31.3227	519.2720	853.0742	27.2351	95
100	0.0520	19.2186	0.0316	0.0016	31.5989	607.2877	879.8540	27.8444	100

Compound Interest Factors

Interest Rate, i	$(1+i)^{-n}$	$(1+i)^n$	$\left[\frac{i(1+i)^n}{(1+i)^n-1}\right]$	$\left[\frac{i}{(1+i)^n-1}\right]$	$\left[\frac{(1+i)^n-1}{i(1+i)^n}\right]$	$\left[\frac{(1+i)^n-1}{i}\right]$	$\left[\frac{(1+i)^n-in-1}{i^2(1+i)^n}\right]$	$\left[\frac{(1+i)^n-in-1}{i(1+i)^n-i}\right]$	
4.00%	Find P	Find F	Find A	Find A	Find P	Find F	Find P	Find A	4.00%
	Know F	Know P	Know P	Know F	Know A	Know A	Know G	Know G	
n	P/F	F/P	A/P	A/F	P/A	F/A	P/G	A/G	n
1	0.9615	1.0400	1.0400	1.0000	0.9615	1.0000	0.0000	0.0000	1
2	0.9246	1.0816	0.5302	0.4902	1.8861	2.0400	0.9246	0.4902	2
3	0.8890	1.1249	0.3603	0.3203	2.7751	3.1216	2.7025	0.9739	3
4	0.8548	1.1699	0.2755	0.2355	3.6299	4.2465	5.2670	1.4510	4
5	0.8219	1.2167	0.2246	0.1846	4.4518	5.4163	8.5547	1.9216	5
6	0.7903	1.2653	0.1908	0.1508	5.2421	6.6330	12.5062	2.3857	6
7	0.7599	1.3159	0.1666	0.1266	6.0021	7.8983	17.0657	2.8433	7
8	0.7307	1.3686	0.1485	0.1085	6.7327	9.2142	22.1806	3.2944	8
9	0.7026	1.4233	0.1345	0.0945	7.4353	10.5828	27.8013	3.7391	9
10	0.6756	1.4802	0.1233	0.0833	8.1109	12.0061	33.8814	4.1773	10
11	0.6496	1.5395	0.1141	0.0741	8.7605	13.4864	40.3772	4.6090	11
12	0.6246	1.6010	0.1066	0.0666	9.3851	15.0258	47.2477	5.0343	12
13	0.6006	1.6651	0.1001	0.0601	9.9856	16.6268	54.4546	5.4533	13
14	0.5775	1.7317	0.0947	0.0547	10.5631	18.2919	61.9618	5.8659	14
15	0.5553	1.8009	0.0899	0.0499	11.1184	20.0236	69.7355	6.2721	15
16	0.5339	1.8730	0.0858	0.0458	11.6523	21.8245	77.7441	6.6720	16
17	0.5134	1.9479	0.0822	0.0422	12.1657	23.6975	85.9581	7.0656	17
18	0.4936	2.0258	0.0790	0.0390	12.6593	25.6454	94.3498	7.4530	18
19	0.4746	2.1068	0.0761	0.0361	13.1339	27.6712	102.8933	7.8342	19
20	0.4564	2.1911	0.0736	0.0336	13.5903	29.7781	111.5647	8.2091	20
21	0.4388	2.2788	0.0713	0.0313	14.0292	31.9692	120.3414	8.5779	21
22	0.4220	2.3699	0.0692	0.0292	14.4511	34.2480	129.2024	8.9407	22
23	0.4057	2.4647	0.0673	0.0273	14.8568	36.6179	138.1284	9.2973	23
24	0.3901	2.5633	0.0656	0.0256	15.2470	39.0826	147.1012	9.6479	24
25	0.3751	2.6658	0.0640	0.0240	15.6221	41.6459	156.1040	9.9925	25
26	0.3607	2.7725	0.0626	0.0226	15.9828	44.3117	165.1212	10.3312	26
27	0.3468	2.8834	0.0612	0.0212	16.3296	47.0842	174.1385	10.6640	27
28	0.3335	2.9987	0.0600	0.0200	16.6631	49.9676	183.1424	10.9909	28
29	0.3207	3.1187	0.0589	0.0189	16.9837	52.9663	192.1206	11.3120	29
30	0.3083	3.2434	0.0578	0.0178	17.2920	56.0849	201.0618	11.6274	30
40	0.2083	4.8010	0.0505	0.0105	19.7928	95.0255	286.5303	14.4765	40
45	0.1712	5.8412	0.0483	0.0083	20.7200	121.0294	325.4028	15.7047	45
50	0.1407	7.1067	0.0466	0.0066	21.4822	152.6671	361.1638	16.8122	50
55	0.1157	8.6464	0.0452	0.0052	22.1086	191.1592	393.6890	17.8070	55
60	0.0951	10.5196	0.0442	0.0042	22.6235	237.9907	422.9966	18.6972	60
65	0.0781	12.7987	0.0434	0.0034	23.0467	294.9684	449.2014	19.4909	65
70	0.0642	15.5716	0.0427	0.0027	23.3945	364.2905	472.4789	20.1961	70
75	0.0528	18.9453	0.0422	0.0022	23.6804	448.6314	493.0408	20.8206	75
80	0.0434	23.0498	0.0418	0.0018	23.9154	551.2450	511.1161	21.3718	80
85	0.0357	28.0436	0.0415	0.0015	24.1085	676.0901	526.9384	21.8569	85
90	0.0293	34.1193	0.0412	0.0012	24.2673	827.9833	540.7369	22.2826	90
95	0.0241	41.5114	0.0410	0.0010	24.3978	1012.7846	552.7307	22.6550	95
100	0.0198	50.5049	0.0408	0.0008	24.5050	1237.6237	563.1249	22.9800	100

Compound Interest Factors

Interest Rate, i	$(1+i)^{-n}$	$(1+i)^{n}$	$\left[\frac{i(1+i)^n}{(1+i)^n-1}\right]$	$\left[\frac{i}{(1+i)^n-1}\right]$	$\left[\frac{(1+i)^n-1}{i(1+i)^n}\right]$	$\left[\frac{(1+i)^n-1}{i}\right]$	$\left[\frac{(1+i)^n-in-1}{i^2(1+i)^n}\right]$	$\left[\frac{(1+i)^n-in-1}{i(1+i)^n-i}\right]$	
5.00%	Find P	Find F	Find A	Find A	Find P	Find F	Find P	Find A	5.00%
	Know F	Know P	Know P	Know F	Know A	Know A	Know G	Know G	
n	P/F	F/P	A/P	A/F	P/A	F/A	P/G	A/G	n
1	0.9524	1.0500	1.0500	1.0000	0.9524	1.0000	0.0000	0.0000	1
2	0.9070	1.1025	0.5378	0.4878	1.8594	2.0500	0.9070	0.4878	2
3	0.8638	1.1576	0.3672	0.3172	2.7232	3.1525	2.6347	0.9675	3
4	0.8227	1.2155	0.2820	0.2320	3.5460	4.3101	5.1028	1.4391	4
5	0.7835	1.2763	0.2310	0.1810	4.3295	5.5256	8.2369	1.9025	5
6	0.7462	1.3401	0.1970	0.1470	5.0757	6.8019	11.9680	2.3579	6
7	0.7107	1.4071	0.1728	0.1228	5.7864	8.1420	16.2321	2.8052	7
8	0.6768	1.4775	0.1547	0.1047	6.4632	9.5491	20.9700	3.2445	8
9	0.6446	1.5513	0.1407	0.0907	7.1078	11.0266	26.1268	3.6758	9
10	0.6139	1.6289	0.1295	0.0795	7.7217	12.5779	31.6520	4.0991	10
11	0.5847	1.7103	0.1204	0.0704	8.3064	14.2068	37.4988	4.5144	11
12	0.5568	1.7959	0.1128	0.0628	8.8633	15.9171	43.6241	4.9219	12
13	0.5303	1.8856	0.1065	0.0565	9.3936	17.7130	49.9879	5.3215	13
14	0.5051	1.9799	0.1010	0.0510	9.8986	19.5986	56.5538	5.7133	14
15	0.4810	2.0789	0.0963	0.0463	10.3797	21.5786	63.2880	6.0973	15
16	0.4581	2.1829	0.0923	0.0423	10.8378	23.6575	70.1597	6.4736	16
17	0.4363	2.2920	0.0887	0.0387	11.2741	25.8404	77.1405	6.8423	17
18	0.4155	2.4066	0.0855	0.0355	11.6896	28.1324	84.2043	7.2034	18
19	0.3957	2.5270	0.0827	0.0327	12.0853	30.5390	91.3275	7.5569	19
20	0.3769	2.6533	0.0802	0.0302	12.4622	33.0660	98.4884	7.9030	20
21	0.3589	2.7860	0.0780	0.0280	12.8212	35.7193	105.6673	8.2416	21
22	0.3418	2.9253	0.0760	0.0260	13.1630	38.5052	112.8461	8.5730	22
23	0.3256	3.0715	0.0741	0.0241	13.4886	41.4305	120.0087	8.8971	23
24	0.3101	3.2251	0.0725	0.0225	13.7986	44.5020	127.1402	9.2140	24
25	0.2953	3.3864	0.0710	0.0210	14.0939	47.7271	134.2275	9.5238	25
26	0.2812	3.5557	0.0696	0.0196	14.3752	51.1135	141.2585	9.8266	26
27	0.2678	3.7335	0.0683	0.0183	14.6430	54.6691	148.2226	10.1224	27
28	0.2551	3.9201	0.0671	0.0171	14.8981	58.4026	155.1101	10.4114	28
29	0.2429	4.1161	0.0660	0.0160	15.1411	62.3227	161.9126	10.6936	29
30	0.2314	4.3219	0.0651	0.0151	15.3725	66.4388	168.6226	10.9691	30
40	0.1420	7.0400	0.0583	0.0083	17.1591	120.7998	229.5452	13.3775	40
45	0.1113	8.9850	0.0563	0.0063	17.7741	159.7002	255.3145	14.3644	45
50	0.0872	11.4674	0.0548	0.0048	18.2559	209.3480	277.9148	15.2233	50
55	0.0683	14.6356	0.0537	0.0037	18.6335	272.7126	297.5104	15.9664	55
60	0.0535	18.6792	0.0528	0.0028	18.9293	353.5837	314.3432	16.6062	60
65	0.0419	23.8399	0.0522	0.0022	19.1611	456.7980	328.6910	17.1541	65
70	0.0329	30.4264	0.0517	0.0017	19.3427	588.5285	340.8409	17.6212	70
75	0.0258	38.8327	0.0513	0.0013	19.4850	756.6537	351.0721	18.0176	75
80	0.0202	49.5614	0.0510	0.0010	19.5965	971.2288	359.6460	18.3526	80
85	0.0158	63.2544	0.0508	0.0008	19.6838	1245.0871	366.8007	18.6346	85
90	0.0124	80.7304	0.0506	0.0006	19.7523	1594.6073	372.7488	18.8712	90
95	0.0097	103.0347	0.0505	0.0005	19.8059	2040.6935	377.6774	19.0689	95
100	0.0076	131.5013	0.0504	0.0004	19.8479	2610.0252	381.7492	19.2337	100

Compound Interest Factors

Interest Rate, i	$(1+i)^{-n}$	$(1+i)^{n}$	$\left[\frac{i(1+i)^n}{(1+i)^n-1}\right]$	$\left[\frac{i}{(1+i)^n-1}\right]$	$\left[\frac{(1+i)^n-1}{i(1+i)^n}\right]$	$\left[\frac{(1+i)^n-1}{i}\right]$	$\left[\frac{(1+i)^n-in-1}{i^2(1+i)^n}\right]$	$\left[\frac{(1+i)^n-in-1}{i(1+i)^n-i}\right]$	
6.00%	Find P	Find F	Find A	Find A	Find P	Find F	Find P	Find A	6.00%
	Know F	Know P	Know P	Know F	Know A	Know A	Know G	Know G	
n	P/F	F/P	A/P	A/F	P/A	F/A	P/G	A/G	n
1	0.9434	1.0600	1.0600	1.0000	0.9434	1.0000	0.0000	0.0000	1
2	0.8900	1.1236	0.5454	0.4854	1.8334	2.0600	0.8900	0.4854	2
3	0.8396	1.1910	0.3741	0.3141	2.6730	3.1836	2.5692	0.9612	3
4	0.7921	1.2625	0.2886	0.2286	3.4651	4.3746	4.9455	1.4272	4
5	0.7473	1.3382	0.2374	0.1774	4.2124	5.6371	7.9345	1.8836	5
6	0.7050	1.4185	0.2034	0.1434	4.9173	6.9753	11.4594	2.3304	6
7	0.6651	1.5036	0.1791	0.1191	5.5824	8.3938	15.4497	2.7676	7
8	0.6274	1.5938	0.1610	0.1010	6.2098	9.8975	19.8416	3.1952	8
9	0.5919	1.6895	0.1470	0.0870	6.8017	11.4913	24.5768	3.6133	9
10	0.5584	1.7908	0.1359	0.0759	7.3601	13.1808	29.6023	4.0220	10
11	0.5268	1.8983	0.1268	0.0668	7.8869	14.9716	34.8702	4.4213	11
12	0.4970	2.0122	0.1193	0.0593	8.3838	16.8699	40.3369	4.8113	12
13	0.4688	2.1329	0.1130	0.0530	8.8527	18.8821	45.9629	5.1920	13
14	0.4423	2.2609	0.1076	0.0476	9.2950	21.0151	51.7128	5.5635	14
15	0.4173	2.3966	0.1030	0.0430	9.7122	23.2760	57.5546	5.9260	15
16	0.3936	2.5404	0.0990	0.0390	10.1059	25.6725	63.4592	6.2794	16
17	0.3714	2.6928	0.0954	0.0354	10.4773	28.2129	69.4011	6.6240	17
18	0.3503	2.8543	0.0924	0.0324	10.8276	30.9057	75.3569	6.9597	18
19	0.3305	3.0256	0.0896	0.0296	11.1581	33.7600	81.3062	7.2867	19
20	0.3118	3.2071	0.0872	0.0272	11.4699	36.7856	87.2304	7.6051	20
21	0.2942	3.3996	0.0850	0.0250	11.7641	39.9927	93.1136	7.9151	21
22	0.2775	3.6035	0.0830	0.0230	12.0416	43.3923	98.9412	8.2166	22
23	0.2618	3.8197	0.0813	0.0213	12.3034	46.9958	104.7007	8.5099	23
24	0.2470	4.0489	0.0797	0.0197	12.5504	50.8156	110.3812	8.7951	24
25	0.2330	4.2919	0.0782	0.0182	12.7834	54.8645	115.9732	9.0722	25
26	0.2198	4.5494	0.0769	0.0169	13.0032	59.1564	121.4684	9.3414	26
27	0.2074	4.8223	0.0757	0.0157	13.2105	63.7058	126.8600	9.6029	27
28	0.1956	5.1117	0.0746	0.0146	13.4062	68.5281	132.1420	9.8568	28
29	0.1846	5.4184	0.0736	0.0136	13.5907	73.6398	137.3096	10.1032	29
30	0.1741	5.7435	0.0726	0.0126	13.7648	79.0582	142.3588	10.3422	30
40	0.0972	10.2857	0.0665	0.0065	15.0463	154.7620	185.9568	12.3590	40
45	0.0727	13.7646	0.0647	0.0047	15.4558	212.7435	203.1096	13.1413	45
50	0.0543	18.4202	0.0634	0.0034	15.7619	290.3359	217.4574	13.7964	50
55	0.0406	24.6503	0.0625	0.0025	15.9905	394.1720	229.3222	14.3411	55
60	0.0303	32.9877	0.0619	0.0019	16.1614	533.1282	239.0428	14.7909	60
65	0.0227	44.1450	0.0614	0.0014	16.2891	719.0829	246.9450	15.1601	65
70	0.0169	59.0759	0.0610	0.0010	16.3845	967.9322	253.3271	15.4613	70
75	0.0126	79.0569	0.0608	0.0008	16.4558	1300.9487	258.4527	15.7058	75
80	0.0095	105.7960	0.0606	0.0006	16.5091	1746.5999	262.5493	15.9033	80
85	0.0071	141.5789	0.0604	0.0004	16.5489	2342.9817	265.8096	16.0620	85
90	0.0053	189.4645	0.0603	0.0003	16.5787	3141.0752	268.3946	16.1891	90
95	0.0039	253.5463	0.0602	0.0002	16.6009	4209.1042	270.4375	16.2905	95
100	0.0029	339.3021	0.0602	0.0002	16.6175	5638.3681	272.0471	16.3711	100

Compound Interest Factors

Interest Rate, i	$(1+i)^{-n}$	$(1+i)^{n}$	$\left[\frac{i(1+i)^n}{(1+i)^n-1}\right]$	$\left[\frac{i}{(1+i)^n-1}\right]$	$\left[\frac{(1+i)^n-1}{i(1+i)^n}\right]$	$\left[\frac{(1+i)^n-1}{i}\right]$	$\left[\frac{(1+i)^n-in-1}{i^2(1+i)^n}\right]$	$\left[\frac{(1+i)^n-in-1}{i(1+i)^n-i}\right]$	
7.00%	Find P	Find F	Find A	Find A	Find P	Find F	Find P	Find A	7.00%
	Know F	Know P	Know P	Know F	Know A	Know A	Know G	Know G	
n	P/F	F/P	A/P	A/F	P/A	F/A	P/G	A/G	n
1	0.9346	1.0700	1.0700	1.0000	0.9346	1.0000	0.0000	0.0000	1
2	0.8734	1.1449	0.5531	0.4831	1.8080	2.0700	0.8734	0.4831	2
3	0.8163	1.2250	0.3811	0.3111	2.6243	3.2149	2.5060	0.9549	3
4	0.7629	1.3108	0.2952	0.2252	3.3872	4.4399	4.7947	1.4155	4
5	0.7130	1.4026	0.2439	0.1739	4.1002	5.7507	7.6467	1.8650	5
6	0.6663	1.5007	0.2098	0.1398	4.7665	7.1533	10.9784	2.3032	6
7	0.6227	1.6058	0.1856	0.1156	5.3893	8.6540	14.7149	2.7304	7
8	0.5820	1.7182	0.1675	0.0975	5.9713	10.2598	18.7889	3.1465	8
9	0.5439	1.8385	0.1535	0.0835	6.5152	11.9780	23.1404	3.5517	9
10	0.5083	1.9672	0.1424	0.0724	7.0236	13.8164	27.7156	3.9461	10
11	0.4751	2.1049	0.1334	0.0634	7.4987	15.7836	32.4665	4.3296	11
12	0.4440	2.2522	0.1259	0.0559	7.9427	17.8885	37.3506	4.7025	12
13	0.4150	2.4098	0.1197	0.0497	8.3577	20.1406	42.3302	5.0648	13
14	0.3878	2.5785	0.1143	0.0443	8.7455	22.5505	47.3718	5.4167	14
15	0.3624	2.7590	0.1098	0.0398	9.1079	25.1290	52.4461	5.7583	15
16	0.3387	2.9522	0.1059	0.0359	9.4466	27.8881	57.5271	6.0897	16
17	0.3166	3.1588	0.1024	0.0324	9.7632	30.8402	62.5923	6.4110	17
18	0.2959	3.3799	0.0994	0.0294	10.0591	33.9990	67.6219	6.7225	18
19	0.2765	3.6165	0.0968	0.0268	10.3356	37.3790	72.5991	7.0242	19
20	0.2584	3.8697	0.0944	0.0244	10.5940	40.9955	77.5091	7.3163	20
21	0.2415	4.1406	0.0923	0.0223	10.8355	44.8652	82.3393	7.5990	21
22	0.2257	4.4304	0.0904	0.0204	11.0612	49.0057	87.0793	7.8725	22
23	0.2109	4.7405	0.0887	0.0187	11.2722	53.4361	91.7201	8.1369	23
24	0.1971	5.0724	0.0872	0.0172	11.4693	58.1767	96.2545	8.3923	24
25	0.1842	5.4274	0.0858	0.0158	11.6536	63.2490	100.6765	8.6391	25
26	0.1722	5.8074	0.0846	0.0146	11.8258	68.6765	104.9814	8.8773	26
27	0.1609	6.2139	0.0834	0.0134	11.9867	74.4838	109.1656	9.1072	27
28	0.1504	6.6488	0.0824	0.0124	12.1371	80.6977	113.2264	9.3289	28
29	0.1406	7.1143	0.0814	0.0114	12.2777	87.3465	117.1622	9.5427	29
30	0.1314	7.6123	0.0806	0.0106	12.4090	94.4608	120.9718	9.7487	30
40	0.0668	14.9745	0.0750	0.0050	13.3317	199.6351	152.2928	11.4233	40
45	0.0476	21.0025	0.0735	0.0035	13.6055	285.7493	163.7559	12.0360	45
50	0.0339	29.4570	0.0725	0.0025	13.8007	406.5289	172.9051	12.5287	50
55	0.0242	41.3150	0.0717	0.0017	13.9399	575.9286	180.1243	12.9215	55
60	0.0173	57.9464	0.0712	0.0012	14.0392	813.5204	185.7677	13.2321	60
65	0.0123	81.2729	0.0709	0.0009	14.1099	1146.7552	190.1452	13.4760	65
70	0.0088	113.9894	0.0706	0.0006	14.1604	1614.1342	193.5185	13.6662	70
75	0.0063	159.8760	0.0704	0.0004	14.1964	2269.6574	196.1035	13.8136	75
80	0.0045	224.2344	0.0703	0.0003	14.2220	3189.0627	198.0748	13.9273	80
85	0.0032	314.5003	0.0702	0.0002	14.2403	4478.5761	199.5717	14.0146	85
90	0.0023	441.1030	0.0702	0.0002	14.2533	6287.1854	200.7042	14.0812	90
95	0.0016	618.6697	0.0701	0.0001	14.2626	8823.8535	201.5581	14.1319	95
100	0.0012	867.7163	0.0701	0.0001	14.2693	##########	202.2001	14.1703	100

Compound Interest Factors

Interest Rate, i	$(1+i)^{-n}$	$(1+i)^{n}$	$\left[\frac{i(1+i)^n}{(1+i)^n-1}\right]$	$\left[\frac{i}{(1+i)^n-1}\right]$	$\left[\frac{(1+i)^n-1}{i(1+i)^n}\right]$	$\left[\frac{(1+i)^n-1}{i}\right]$	$\left[\frac{(1+i)^n-in-1}{i^2(1+i)^n}\right]$	$\left[\frac{(1+i)^n-in-1}{i(1+i)^n-i}\right]$	
8.00%	Find P	Find F	Find A	Find A	Find P	Find F	Find P	Find A	8.00%
	Know F	Know P	Know P	Know F	Know A	Know A	Know G	Know G	
n	P/F	F/P	A/P	A/F	P/A	F/A	P/G	A/G	n
1	0.9259	1.0800	1.0800	1.0000	0.9259	1.0000	0.0000	0.0000	1
2	0.8573	1.1664	0.5608	0.4808	1.7833	2.0800	0.8573	0.4808	2
3	0.7938	1.2597	0.3880	0.3080	2.5771	3.2464	2.4450	0.9487	3
4	0.7350	1.3605	0.3019	0.2219	3.3121	4.5061	4.6501	1.4040	4
5	0.6806	1.4693	0.2505	0.1705	3.9927	5.8666	7.3724	1.8465	5
6	0.6302	1.5869	0.2163	0.1363	4.6229	7.3359	10.5233	2.2763	6
7	0.5835	1.7138	0.1921	0.1121	5.2064	8.9228	14.0242	2.6937	7
8	0.5403	1.8509	0.1740	0.0940	5.7466	10.6366	17.8061	3.0985	8
9	0.5002	1.9990	0.1601	0.0801	6.2469	12.4876	21.8081	3.4910	9
10	0.4632	2.1589	0.1490	0.0690	6.7101	14.4866	25.9768	3.8713	10
11	0.4289	2.3316	0.1401	0.0601	7.1390	16.6455	30.2657	4.2395	11
12	0.3971	2.5182	0.1327	0.0527	7.5361	18.9771	34.6339	4.5957	12
13	0.3677	2.7196	0.1265	0.0465	7.9038	21.4953	39.0463	4.9402	13
14	0.3405	2.9372	0.1213	0.0413	8.2442	24.2149	43.4723	5.2731	14
15	0.3152	3.1722	0.1168	0.0368	8.5595	27.1521	47.8857	5.5945	15
16	0.2919	3.4259	0.1130	0.0330	8.8514	30.3243	52.2640	5.9046	16
17	0.2703	3.7000	0.1096	0.0296	9.1216	33.7502	56.5883	6.2037	17
18	0.2502	3.9960	0.1067	0.0267	9.3719	37.4502	60.8426	6.4920	18
19	0.2317	4.3157	0.1041	0.0241	9.6036	41.4463	65.0134	6.7697	19
20	0.2145	4.6610	0.1019	0.0219	9.8181	45.7620	69.0898	7.0369	20
21	0.1987	5.0338	0.0998	0.0198	10.0168	50.4229	73.0629	7.2940	21
22	0.1839	5.4365	0.0980	0.0180	10.2007	55.4568	76.9257	7.5412	22
23	0.1703	5.8715	0.0964	0.0164	10.3711	60.8933	80.6726	7.7786	23
24	0.1577	6.3412	0.0950	0.0150	10.5288	66.7648	84.2997	8.0066	24
25	0.1460	6.8485	0.0937	0.0137	10.6748	73.1059	87.8041	8.2254	25
26	0.1352	7.3964	0.0925	0.0125	10.8100	79.9544	91.1842	8.4352	26
27	0.1252	7.9881	0.0914	0.0114	10.9352	87.3508	94.4390	8.6363	27
28	0.1159	8.6271	0.0905	0.0105	11.0511	95.3388	97.5687	8.8289	28
29	0.1073	9.3173	0.0896	0.0096	11.1584	103.9659	100.5738	9.0133	29
30	0.0994	10.0627	0.0888	0.0088	11.2578	113.2832	103.4558	9.1897	30
40	0.046	21.725	0.084	0.004	11.925	259.057	126.042	10.570	40
45	0.031	31.920	0.083	0.003	12.108	386.506	133.733	11.045	45
50	0.021	46.902	0.082	0.002	12.233	573.770	139.593	11.411	50
55	0.015	68.914	0.081	0.001	12.319	848.923	144.006	11.690	55
60	0.010	101.257	0.081	0.001	12.377	1253.213	147.300	11.902	60
65	0.007	148.780	0.081	0.001	12.416	1847.248	149.739	12.060	65
70	0.005	218.606	0.080	0.000	12.443	2720.080	151.533	12.178	70
75	0.003	321.205	0.080	0.000	12.461	4002.557	152.845	12.266	75
80	0.002	471.955	0.080	0.000	12.474	5886.935	153.800	12.330	80
85	0.001	693.456	0.080	0.000	12.482	8655.706	154.492	12.377	85
90	0.001	1018.915	0.080	0.000	12.488	12723.939	154.993	12.412	90
95	0.001	1497.121	0.080	0.000	12.492	18701.507	155.352	12.437	95
100	0.000	2199.761	0.080	0.000	12.494	27484.516	155.611	12.455	100

Compound Interest Factors

Interest Rate, i	$(1+i)^{-n}$	$(1+i)^{n}$	$\left[\frac{i(1+i)^n}{(1+i)^n-1}\right]$	$\left[\frac{i}{(1+i)^n-1}\right]$	$\left[\frac{(1+i)^n-1}{i(1+i)^n}\right]$	$\left[\frac{(1+i)^n-1}{i}\right]$	$\left[\frac{(1+i)^n-in-1}{i^2(1+i)^n}\right]$	$\left[\frac{(1+i)^n-in-1}{i(1+i)^n-i}\right]$	
9.00%	Find P	Find F	Find A	Find A	Find P	Find F	Find P	Find A	9.00%
	Know F	Know P	Know P	Know F	Know A	Know A	Know G	Know G	
n	P/F	F/P	A/P	A/F	P/A	F/A	P/G	A/G	n
1	0.9174	1.0900	1.0900	1.0000	0.9174	1.0000	0.0000	0.0000	1
2	0.8417	1.1881	0.5685	0.4785	1.7591	2.0900	0.8417	0.4785	2
3	0.7722	1.2950	0.3951	0.3051	2.5313	3.2781	2.3860	0.9426	3
4	0.7084	1.4116	0.3087	0.2187	3.2397	4.5731	4.5113	1.3925	4
5	0.6499	1.5386	0.2571	0.1671	3.8897	5.9847	7.1110	1.8282	5
6	0.5963	1.6771	0.2229	0.1329	4.4859	7.5233	10.0924	2.2498	6
7	0.5470	1.8280	0.1987	0.1087	5.0330	9.2004	13.3746	2.6574	7
8	0.5019	1.9926	0.1807	0.0907	5.5348	11.0285	16.8877	3.0512	8
9	0.4604	2.1719	0.1668	0.0768	5.9952	13.0210	20.5711	3.4312	9
10	0.4224	2.3674	0.1558	0.0658	6.4177	15.1929	24.3728	3.7978	10
11	0.3875	2.5804	0.1469	0.0569	6.8052	17.5603	28.2481	4.1510	11
12	0.3555	2.8127	0.1397	0.0497	7.1607	20.1407	32.1590	4.4910	12
13	0.3262	3.0658	0.1336	0.0436	7.4869	22.9534	36.0731	4.8182	13
14	0.2992	3.3417	0.1284	0.0384	7.7862	26.0192	39.9633	5.1326	14
15	0.2745	3.6425	0.1241	0.0341	8.0607	29.3609	43.8069	5.4346	15
16	0.2519	3.9703	0.1203	0.0303	8.3126	33.0034	47.5849	5.7245	16
17	0.2311	4.3276	0.1170	0.0270	8.5436	36.9737	51.2821	6.0024	17
18	0.2120	4.7171	0.1142	0.0242	8.7556	41.3013	54.8860	6.2687	18
19	0.1945	5.1417	0.1117	0.0217	8.9501	46.0185	58.3868	6.5236	19
20	0.1784	5.6044	0.1095	0.0195	9.1285	51.1601	61.7770	6.7674	20
21	0.1637	6.1088	0.1076	0.0176	9.2922	56.7645	65.0509	7.0006	21
22	0.1502	6.6586	0.1059	0.0159	9.4424	62.8733	68.2048	7.2232	22
23	0.1378	7.2579	0.1044	0.0144	9.5802	69.5319	71.2359	7.4357	23
24	0.1264	7.9111	0.1030	0.0130	9.7066	76.7898	74.1433	7.6384	24
25	0.1160	8.6231	0.1018	0.0118	9.8226	84.7009	76.9265	7.8316	25
26	0.1064	9.3992	0.1007	0.0107	9.9290	93.3240	79.5863	8.0156	26
27	0.0976	10.2451	0.0997	0.0097	10.0266	102.7231	82.1241	8.1906	27
28	0.0895	11.1671	0.0989	0.0089	10.1161	112.9682	84.5419	8.3571	28
29	0.0822	12.1722	0.0981	0.0081	10.1983	124.1354	86.8422	8.5154	29
30	0.0754	13.2677	0.0973	0.0073	10.2737	136.3075	89.0280	8.6657	30
40	0.032	31.409	0.093	0.003	10.757	337.882	105.376	9.796	40
45	0.021	48.327	0.092	0.002	10.881	525.859	110.556	10.160	45
50	0.013	74.358	0.091	0.001	10.962	815.084	114.325	10.430	50
55	0.009	114.408	0.091	0.001	11.014	1260.092	117.036	10.626	55
60	0.006	176.031	0.091	0.001	11.048	1944.792	118.968	10.768	60
65	0.004	270.846	0.090	0.000	11.070	2998.288	120.334	10.870	65
70	0.002	416.730	0.090	0.000	11.084	4619.223	121.294	10.943	70
75	0.002	641.191	0.090	0.000	11.094	7113.232	121.965	10.994	75
80	0.001	986.552	0.090	0.000	11.100	10950.574	122.431	11.030	80
85	0.001	1517.932	0.090	0.000	11.104	16854.800	122.753	11.055	85
90	0.000	2335.527	0.090	0.000	11.106	25939.184	122.976	11.073	90
95	0.000	3593.497	0.090	0.000	11.108	39916.635	123.129	11.085	95
100	0.000	5529.041	0.090	0.000	11.109	61422.675	123.234	11.093	100

Compound Interest Factors

Interest Rate, i	$(1+i)^{-n}$	$(1+i)^{n}$	$\left[\frac{i(1+i)^n}{(1+i)^n-1}\right]$	$\left[\frac{i}{(1+i)^n-1}\right]$	$\left[\frac{(1+i)^n-1}{i(1+i)^n}\right]$	$\left[\frac{(1+i)^n-1}{i}\right]$	$\left[\frac{(1+i)^n-in-1}{i^2(1+i)^n}\right]$	$\left[\frac{(1+i)^n-in-1}{i(1+i)^n-i}\right]$	
10.00%	Find P	Find F	Find A	Find A	Find P	Find F	Find P	Find A	10.00%
	Know F	Know P	Know P	Know F	Know A	Know A	Know G	Know G	
n	P/F	F/P	A/P	A/F	P/A	F/A	P/G	A/G	n
1	0.9091	1.1000	1.1000	1.0000	0.9091	1.0000	0.0000	0.0000	1
2	0.8264	1.2100	0.5762	0.4762	1.7355	2.1000	0.8264	0.4762	2
3	0.7513	1.3310	0.4021	0.3021	2.4869	3.3100	2.3291	0.9366	3
4	0.6830	1.4641	0.3155	0.2155	3.1699	4.6410	4.3781	1.3812	4
5	0.6209	1.6105	0.2638	0.1638	3.7908	6.1051	6.8618	1.8101	5
6	0.5645	1.7716	0.2296	0.1296	4.3553	7.7156	9.6842	2.2236	6
7	0.5132	1.9487	0.2054	0.1054	4.8684	9.4872	12.7631	2.6216	7
8	0.4665	2.1436	0.1874	0.0874	5.3349	11.4359	16.0287	3.0045	8
9	0.4241	2.3579	0.1736	0.0736	5.7590	13.5795	19.4215	3.3724	9
10	0.3855	2.5937	0.1627	0.0627	6.1446	15.9374	22.8913	3.7255	10
11	0.3505	2.8531	0.1540	0.0540	6.4951	18.5312	26.3963	4.0641	11
12	0.3186	3.1384	0.1468	0.0468	6.8137	21.3843	29.9012	4.3884	12
13	0.2897	3.4523	0.1408	0.0408	7.1034	24.5227	33.3772	4.6988	13
14	0.2633	3.7975	0.1357	0.0357	7.3667	27.9750	36.8005	4.9955	14
15	0.2394	4.1772	0.1315	0.0315	7.6061	31.7725	40.1520	5.2789	15
16	0.2176	4.5950	0.1278	0.0278	7.8237	35.9497	43.4164	5.5493	16
17	0.1978	5.0545	0.1247	0.0247	8.0216	40.5447	46.5819	5.8071	17
18	0.1799	5.5599	0.1219	0.0219	8.2014	45.5992	49.6395	6.0526	18
19	0.1635	6.1159	0.1195	0.0195	8.3649	51.1591	52.5827	6.2861	19
20	0.1486	6.7275	0.1175	0.0175	8.5136	57.2750	55.4069	6.5081	20
21	0.1351	7.4002	0.1156	0.0156	8.6487	64.0025	58.1095	6.7189	21
22	0.1228	8.1403	0.1140	0.0140	8.7715	71.4027	60.6893	6.9189	22
23	0.1117	8.9543	0.1126	0.0126	8.8832	79.5430	63.1462	7.1085	23
24	0.1015	9.8497	0.1113	0.0113	8.9847	88.4973	65.4813	7.2881	24
25	0.0923	10.8347	0.1102	0.0102	9.0770	98.3471	67.6964	7.4580	25
26	0.0839	11.9182	0.1092	0.0092	9.1609	109.1818	69.7940	7.6186	26
27	0.0763	13.1100	0.1083	0.0083	9.2372	121.0999	71.7773	7.7704	27
28	0.0693	14.4210	0.1075	0.0075	9.3066	134.2099	73.6495	7.9137	28
29	0.0630	15.8631	0.1067	0.0067	9.3696	148.6309	75.4146	8.0489	29
30	0.0573	17.4494	0.1061	0.0061	9.4269	164.4940	77.0766	8.1762	30
40	0.022	45.259	0.102	0.002	9.779	442.593	88.953	9.096	40
45	0.014	72.890	0.101	0.001	9.863	718.905	92.454	9.374	45
50	0.009	117.391	0.101	0.001	9.915	1163.909	94.889	9.570	50
55	0.005	189.059	0.101	0.001	9.947	1880.591	96.562	9.708	55
60	0.003	304.482	0.100	0.000	9.967	3034.82	97.701	9.802	60
65	0.002	490.371	0.100	0.000	9.980	4893.71	98.471	9.867	65
70	0.001	789.747	0.100	0.000	9.987	7887.47	98.987	9.911	70
75	0.001	1271.895	0.100	0.000	9.992	12708.95	99.332	9.941	75
80	0.000	2048.400	0.100	0.000	9.995	20474.00	99.561	9.961	80
85	0.000	3298.969	0.100	0.000	9.997	32979.69	99.712	9.974	85
90	0.000	5313.023	0.100	0.000	9.998	53120.23	99.812	9.983	90
95	0.000	8556.676	0.100	0.000	9.999	85556.76	99.877	9.989	95
100	0.000	13780.612	0.100	0.000	9.999	137796.12	99.920	9.993	100

Compound Interest Factors

Interest Rate, i	$(1+i)^{-n}$	$(1+i)^{n}$	$\left[\frac{i(1+i)^n}{(1+i)^n-1}\right]$	$\left[\frac{i}{(1+i)^n-1}\right]$	$\left[\frac{(1+i)^n-1}{i(1+i)^n}\right]$	$\left[\frac{(1+i)^n-1}{i}\right]$	$\left[\frac{(1+i)^n-in-1}{i^2(1+i)^n}\right]$	$\left[\frac{(1+i)^n-in-1}{i(1+i)^n-i}\right]$	
12.00%	Find P	Find F	Find A	Find A	Find P	Find F	Find P	Find A	12.00%
	Know F	Know P	Know P	Know F	Know A	Know A	Know G	Know G	
n	P/F	F/P	A/P	A/F	P/A	F/A	P/G	A/G	n
1	0.8929	1.1200	1.1200	1.0000	0.8929	1.0000	0.0000	0.0000	1
2	0.7972	1.2544	0.5917	0.4717	1.6901	2.1200	0.7972	0.4717	2
3	0.7118	1.4049	0.4163	0.2963	2.4018	3.3744	2.2208	0.9246	3
4	0.6355	1.5735	0.3292	0.2092	3.0373	4.7793	4.1273	1.3589	4
5	0.5674	1.7623	0.2774	0.1574	3.6048	6.3528	6.3970	1.7746	5
6	0.5066	1.9738	0.2432	0.1232	4.1114	8.1152	8.9302	2.1720	6
7	0.4523	2.2107	0.2191	0.0991	4.5638	10.0890	11.6443	2.5515	7
8	0.4039	2.4760	0.2013	0.0813	4.9676	12.2997	14.4714	2.9131	8
9	0.3606	2.7731	0.1877	0.0677	5.3282	14.7757	17.3563	3.2574	9
10	0.3220	3.1058	0.1770	0.0570	5.6502	17.5487	20.2541	3.5847	10
11	0.2875	3.4785	0.1684	0.0484	5.9377	20.6546	23.1288	3.8953	11
12	0.2567	3.8960	0.1614	0.0414	6.1944	24.1331	25.9523	4.1897	12
13	0.2292	4.3635	0.1557	0.0357	6.4235	28.0291	28.7024	4.4683	13
14	0.2046	4.8871	0.1509	0.0309	6.6282	32.3926	31.3624	4.7317	14
15	0.1827	5.4736	0.1468	0.0268	6.8109	37.2797	33.9202	4.9803	15
16	0.1631	6.1304	0.1434	0.0234	6.9740	42.7533	36.3670	5.2147	16
17	0.1456	6.8660	0.1405	0.0205	7.1196	48.8837	38.6973	5.4353	17
18	0.1300	7.6900	0.1379	0.0179	7.2497	55.7497	40.9080	5.6427	18
19	0.1161	8.6128	0.1358	0.0158	7.3658	63.4397	42.9979	5.8375	19
20	0.1037	9.6463	0.1339	0.0139	7.4694	72.0524	44.9676	6.0202	20
21	0.0926	10.8038	0.1322	0.0122	7.5620	81.6987	46.8188	6.1913	21
22	0.0826	12.1003	0.1308	0.0108	7.6446	92.5026	48.5543	6.3514	22
23	0.0738	13.5523	0.1296	0.0096	7.7184	104.6029	50.1776	6.5010	23
24	0.0659	15.1786	0.1285	0.0085	7.7843	118.1552	51.6929	6.6406	24
25	0.0588	17.0001	0.1275	0.0075	7.8431	133.3339	53.1046	6.7708	25
26	0.0525	19.0401	0.1267	0.0067	7.8957	150.3339	54.4177	6.8921	26
27	0.0469	21.3249	0.1259	0.0059	7.9426	169.3740	55.6369	7.0049	27
28	0.0419	23.8839	0.1252	0.0052	7.9844	190.6989	56.7674	7.1098	28
29	0.0374	26.7499	0.1247	0.0047	8.0218	214.5828	57.8141	7.2071	29
30	0.0334	29.9599	0.1241	0.0041	8.0552	241.3327	58.7821	7.2974	30
40	0.011	93.051	0.121	0.001	8.244	767.091	65.116	7.899	40
45	0.006	163.988	0.121	0.001	8.283	1358.230	66.734	8.057	45
50	0.003	289.002	0.120	0.000	8.304	2400.018	67.762	8.160	50
55	0.002	509.321	0.120	0.000	8.317	4236.005	68.408	8.225	55
60	0.001	897.597	0.120	0.000	8.324	7471.64	68.810	8.266	60
65	0.001	1581.872	0.120	0.000	8.328	13173.94	69.058	8.292	65
70	0.000	2787.800	0.120	0.000	8.330	23223.33	69.210	8.308	70
75	0.000	4913.056	0.120	0.000	8.332	40933.80	69.303	8.318	75
80	0.000	8658.483	0.120	0.000	8.332	72145.69	69.359	8.324	80
85	0.000	15259.206	0.120	0.000	8.333	127151.71	69.393	8.328	85
90	0.000	26891.934	0.120	0.000	8.333	224091.12	69.414	8.330	90
95	0.000	47392.777	0.120	0.000	8.333	394931.47	69.426	8.331	95
100	0.000	83522.266	0.120	0.000	8.333	696010.55	69.434	8.332	100

Compound Interest Factors

Interest Rate, i	$(1+i)^{-n}$	$(1+i)^{n}$	$\left[\frac{i(1+i)^n}{(1+i)^n-1}\right]$	$\left[\frac{i}{(1+i)^n-1}\right]$	$\left[\frac{(1+i)^n-1}{i(1+i)^n}\right]$	$\left[\frac{(1+i)^n-1}{i}\right]$	$\left[\frac{(1+i)^n-in-1}{i^2(1+i)^n}\right]$	$\left[\frac{(1+i)^n-in-1}{i(1+i)^n-i}\right]$	
14.00%	Find P	Find F	Find A	Find A	Find P	Find F	Find P	Find A	14.00%
	Know F	Know P	Know P	Know F	Know A	Know A	Know G	Know G	
n	P/F	F/P	A/P	A/F	P/A	F/A	P/G	A/G	n
1	0.8772	1.1400	1.1400	1.0000	0.8772	1.0000	0.0000	0.0000	1
2	0.7695	1.2996	0.6073	0.4673	1.6467	2.1400	0.7695	0.4673	2
3	0.6750	1.4815	0.4307	0.2907	2.3216	3.4396	2.1194	0.9129	3
4	0.5921	1.6890	0.3432	0.2032	2.9137	4.9211	3.8957	1.3370	4
5	0.5194	1.9254	0.2913	0.1513	3.4331	6.6101	5.9731	1.7399	5
6	0.4556	2.1950	0.2572	0.1172	3.8887	8.5355	8.2511	2.1218	6
7	0.3996	2.5023	0.2332	0.0932	4.2883	10.7305	10.6489	2.4832	7
8	0.3506	2.8526	0.2156	0.0756	4.6389	13.2328	13.1028	2.8246	8
9	0.3075	3.2519	0.2022	0.0622	4.9464	16.0853	15.5629	3.1463	9
10	0.2697	3.7072	0.1917	0.0517	5.2161	19.3373	17.9906	3.4490	10
11	0.2366	4.2262	0.1834	0.0434	5.4527	23.0445	20.3567	3.7333	11
12	0.2076	4.8179	0.1767	0.0367	5.6603	27.2707	22.6399	3.9998	12
13	0.1821	5.4924	0.1712	0.0312	5.8424	32.0887	24.8247	4.2491	13
14	0.1597	6.2613	0.1666	0.0266	6.0021	37.5811	26.9009	4.4819	14
15	0.1401	7.1379	0.1628	0.0228	6.1422	43.8424	28.8623	4.6990	15
16	0.1229	8.1372	0.1596	0.0196	6.2651	50.9804	30.7057	4.9011	16
17	0.1078	9.2765	0.1569	0.0169	6.3729	59.1176	32.4305	5.0888	17
18	0.0946	10.5752	0.1546	0.0146	6.4674	68.3941	34.0380	5.2630	18
19	0.0829	12.0557	0.1527	0.0127	6.5504	78.9692	35.5311	5.4243	19
20	0.0728	13.7435	0.1510	0.0110	6.6231	91.0249	36.9135	5.5734	20
21	0.0638	15.6676	0.1495	0.0095	6.6870	104.7684	38.1901	5.7111	21
22	0.0560	17.8610	0.1483	0.0083	6.7429	120.4360	39.3658	5.8381	22
23	0.0491	20.3616	0.1472	0.0072	6.7921	138.2970	40.4463	5.9549	23
24	0.0431	23.2122	0.1463	0.0063	6.8351	158.6586	41.4371	6.0624	24
25	0.0378	26.4619	0.1455	0.0055	6.8729	181.8708	42.3441	6.1610	25
26	0.0331	30.1666	0.1448	0.0048	6.9061	208.3327	43.1728	6.2514	26
27	0.0291	34.3899	0.1442	0.0042	6.9352	238.4993	43.9289	6.3342	27
28	0.0255	39.2045	0.1437	0.0037	6.9607	272.8892	44.6176	6.4100	28
29	0.0224	44.6931	0.1432	0.0032	6.9830	312.0937	45.2441	6.4791	29
30	0.0196	50.9502	0.1428	0.0028	7.0027	356.7868	45.8132	6.5423	30
40	0.01	188.88	0.14	0.00	7.11	1342.0	49.24	6.93	40
45	0.00	363.68	0.14	0.00	7.12	2590.6	50.00	7.02	45
50	0.00	700.23	0.14	0.00	7.13	4994.5	50.44	7.07	50
55	0.00	1348.24	0.14	0.00	7.14	9623.1	50.69	7.10	55
60	0.00	2595.92	0.14	0.00	7.14	18535.1	50.84	7.12	60
65	0.00	4998.22	0.14	0.00	7.14	35694.4	50.92	7.13	65
70	0.00	9623.64	0.14	0.00	7.14	68733.2	50.96	7.14	70
75	0.00	18529.51	0.14	0.00	7.14	132346.5	50.99	7.14	75
80	0.00	35676.98	0.14	0.00	7.14	254828.4	51.00	7.14	80
85	0.00	68692.98	0.14	0.00	7.14	490657.0	51.01	7.14	85
90	0.00	132262.47	0.14	0.00	7.14	944724.8	51.02	7.14	90
95	0.00	254660.08	0.14	0.00	7.14	1818993.5	51.02	7.14	95
100	0.00	490326.24	0.14	0.00	7.14	3502323.1	51.02	7.14	100

Compound Interest Factors

Interest Rate, i	$(1+i)^{-n}$	$(1+i)^n$	$\left[\frac{i(1+i)^n}{(1+i)^n-1}\right]$	$\left[\frac{i}{(1+i)^n-1}\right]$	$\left[\frac{(1+i)^n-1}{i(1+i)^n}\right]$	$\left[\frac{(1+i)^n-1}{i}\right]$	$\left[\frac{(1+i)^n-in-1}{i^2(1+i)^n}\right]$	$\left[\frac{(1+i)^n-in-1}{i(1+i)^n-i}\right]$	
15.00%	Find P	Find F	Find A	Find A	Find P	Find F	Find P	Find A	15.00%
	Know F	Know P	Know P	Know F	Know A	Know A	Know G	Know G	
n	P/F	F/P	A/P	A/F	P/A	F/A	P/G	A/G	n
1	0.8696	1.1500	1.1500	1.0000	0.8696	1.0000	0.0000	0.0000	1
2	0.7561	1.3225	0.6151	0.4651	1.6257	2.1500	0.7561	0.4651	2
3	0.6575	1.5209	0.4380	0.2880	2.2832	3.4725	2.0712	0.9071	3
4	0.5718	1.7490	0.3503	0.2003	2.8550	4.9934	3.7864	1.3263	4
5	0.4972	2.0114	0.2983	0.1483	3.3522	6.7424	5.7751	1.7228	5
6	0.4323	2.3131	0.2642	0.1142	3.7845	8.7537	7.9368	2.0972	6
7	0.3759	2.6600	0.2404	0.0904	4.1604	11.0668	10.1924	2.4498	7
8	0.3269	3.0590	0.2229	0.0729	4.4873	13.7268	12.4807	2.7813	8
9	0.2843	3.5179	0.2096	0.0596	4.7716	16.7858	14.7548	3.0922	9
10	0.2472	4.0456	0.1993	0.0493	5.0188	20.3037	16.9795	3.3832	10
11	0.2149	4.6524	0.1911	0.0411	5.2337	24.3493	19.1289	3.6549	11
12	0.1869	5.3503	0.1845	0.0345	5.4206	29.0017	21.1849	3.9082	12
13	0.1625	6.1528	0.1791	0.0291	5.5831	34.3519	23.1352	4.1438	13
14	0.1413	7.0757	0.1747	0.0247	5.7245	40.5047	24.9725	4.3624	14
15	0.1229	8.1371	0.1710	0.0210	5.8474	47.5804	26.6930	4.5650	15
16	0.1069	9.3576	0.1679	0.0179	5.9542	55.7175	28.2960	4.7522	16
17	0.0929	10.7613	0.1654	0.0154	6.0472	65.0751	29.7828	4.9251	17
18	0.0808	12.3755	0.1632	0.0132	6.1280	75.8364	31.1565	5.0843	18
19	0.0703	14.2318	0.1613	0.0113	6.1982	88.2118	32.4213	5.2307	19
20	0.0611	16.3665	0.1598	0.0098	6.2593	102.4436	33.5822	5.3651	20
21	0.0531	18.8215	0.1584	0.0084	6.3125	118.8101	34.6448	5.4883	21
22	0.0462	21.6447	0.1573	0.0073	6.3587	137.6316	35.6150	5.6010	22
23	0.0402	24.8915	0.1563	0.0063	6.3988	159.2764	36.4988	5.7040	23
24	0.0349	28.6252	0.1554	0.0054	6.4338	184.1678	37.3023	5.7979	24
25	0.0304	32.9190	0.1547	0.0047	6.4641	212.7930	38.0314	5.8834	25
26	0.0264	37.8568	0.1541	0.0041	6.4906	245.7120	38.6918	5.9612	26
27	0.0230	43.5353	0.1535	0.0035	6.5135	283.5688	39.2890	6.0319	27
28	0.0200	50.0656	0.1531	0.0031	6.5335	327.1041	39.8283	6.0960	28
29	0.0174	57.5755	0.1527	0.0027	6.5509	377.1697	40.3146	6.1541	29
30	0.0151	66.2118	0.1523	0.0023	6.5660	434.7451	40.7526	6.2066	30
40	0.00	267.9	0.15	0.00	6.64	1779.1	43.28	6.52	40
45	0.00	538.8	0.15	0.00	6.65	3585.1	43.81	6.58	45
50	0.00	1083.7	0.15	0.00	6.66	7217.7	44.10	6.62	50
55	0.00	2179.6	0.15	0.00	6.66	14524.1	44.26	6.64	55
60	0.00	4384.0	0.15	0.00	6.67	29220.0	44.34	6.65	60
65	0.00	8817.8	0.15	0.00	6.67	58778.6	44.39	6.66	65
70	0.00	17735.7	0.15	0.00	6.67	118231.5	44.42	6.66	70
75	0.00	35672.9	0.15	0.00	6.67	237812.5	44.43	6.66	75
80	0.00	71750.9	0.15	0.00	6.67	478332.5	44.44	6.67	80
85	0.00	144316.6	0.15	0.00	6.67	962104.3	44.44	6.67	85
90	0.00	290272.3	0.15	0.00	6.67	1935142.2	44.44	6.67	90
95	0.00	583841.3	0.15	0.00	6.67	3892268.9	44.44	6.67	95
100	0.00	1174313.5	0.15	0.00	6.67	7828749.7	44.44	6.67	100

Compound Interest Factors

Interest Rate, i	$(1+i)^{-n}$	$(1+i)^n$	$\left[\frac{i(1+i)^n}{(1+i)^n-1}\right]$	$\left[\frac{i}{(1+i)^n-1}\right]$	$\left[\frac{(1+i)^n-1}{i(1+i)^n}\right]$	$\left[\frac{(1+i)^n-1}{i}\right]$	$\left[\frac{(1+i)^n-in-1}{i^2(1+i)^n}\right]$	$\left[\frac{(1+i)^n-in-1}{i(1+i)^n-i}\right]$	
20.00%	Find P	Find F	Find A	Find A	Find P	Find F	Find P	Find A	20.00%
	Know F	Know P	Know P	Know F	Know A	Know A	Know G	Know G	
n	P/F	F/P	A/P	A/F	P/A	F/A	P/G	A/G	n
1	0.8333	1.2000	1.2000	1.0000	0.8333	1.0000	0.0000	0.0000	1
2	0.6944	1.4400	0.6545	0.4545	1.5278	2.2000	0.6944	0.4545	2
3	0.5787	1.7280	0.4747	0.2747	2.1065	3.6400	1.8519	0.8791	3
4	0.4823	2.0736	0.3863	0.1863	2.5887	5.3680	3.2986	1.2742	4
5	0.4019	2.4883	0.3344	0.1344	2.9906	7.4416	4.9061	1.6405	5
6	0.3349	2.9860	0.3007	0.1007	3.3255	9.9299	6.5806	1.9788	6
7	0.2791	3.5832	0.2774	0.0774	3.6046	12.9159	8.2551	2.2902	7
8	0.2326	4.2998	0.2606	0.0606	3.8372	16.4991	9.8831	2.5756	8
9	0.1938	5.1598	0.2481	0.0481	4.0310	20.7989	11.4335	2.8364	9
10	0.1615	6.1917	0.2385	0.0385	4.1925	25.9587	12.8871	3.0739	10
11	0.1346	7.4301	0.2311	0.0311	4.3271	32.1504	14.2330	3.2893	11
12	0.1122	8.9161	0.2253	0.0253	4.4392	39.5805	15.4667	3.4841	12
13	0.0935	10.6993	0.2206	0.0206	4.5327	48.4966	16.5883	3.6597	13
14	0.0779	12.8392	0.2169	0.0169	4.6106	59.1959	17.6008	3.8175	14
15	0.0649	15.4070	0.2139	0.0139	4.6755	72.0351	18.5095	3.9588	15
16	0.0541	18.4884	0.2114	0.0114	4.7296	87.4421	19.3208	4.0851	16
17	0.0451	22.1861	0.2094	0.0094	4.7746	105.9306	20.0419	4.1976	17
18	0.0376	26.6233	0.2078	0.0078	4.8122	128.1167	20.6805	4.2975	18
19	0.0313	31.9480	0.2065	0.0065	4.8435	154.7400	21.2439	4.3861	19
20	0.0261	38.3376	0.2054	0.0054	4.8696	186.6880	21.7395	4.4643	20
21	0.0217	46.0051	0.2044	0.0044	4.8913	225.0256	22.1742	4.5334	21
22	0.0181	55.2061	0.2037	0.0037	4.9094	271.0307	22.5546	4.5941	22
23	0.0151	66.2474	0.2031	0.0031	4.9245	326.2369	22.8867	4.6475	23
24	0.0126	79.4968	0.2025	0.0025	4.9371	392.4842	23.1760	4.6943	24
25	0.0105	95.3962	0.2021	0.0021	4.9476	471.9811	23.4276	4.7352	25
26	0.0087	114.4755	0.2018	0.0018	4.9563	567.3773	23.6460	4.7709	26
27	0.0073	137.3706	0.2015	0.0015	4.9636	681.8528	23.8353	4.8020	27
28	0.0061	164.8447	0.2012	0.0012	4.9697	819.2233	23.9991	4.8291	28
29	0.0051	197.8136	0.2010	0.0010	4.9747	984.0680	24.1406	4.8527	29
30	0.0042	237.3763	0.2008	0.0008	4.9789	1181.8816	24.2628	4.8731	30
40	0.00	1469.8	0.20	0.00	5.00	7344	24.85	4.97	40
45	0.00	3657.3	0.20	0.00	5.00	18281	24.93	4.99	45
50	0.00	9100.4	0.20	0.00	5.00	45497	24.97	4.99	50
55	0.00	22644.8	0.20	0.00	5.00	113219	24.99	5.00	55
60	0.00	56347.5	0.20	0.00	5.00	281733	24.99	5.00	60
65	0.00	140210.6	0.20	0.00	5.00	701048	25.00	5.00	65
70	0.00	348889	0.20	0.00	5.00	1744440	25.00	5.00	70
75	0.00	868147	0.20	0.00	5.00	4340732	25.00	5.00	75
80	0.00	2160228	0.20	0.00	5.00	10801137	25.00	5.00	80
85	0.00	5375340	0.20	0.00	5.00	26876693	25.00	5.00	85
90	0.00	13375565	0.20	0.00	5.00	66877821	25.00	5.00	90
95	0.00	33282687	0.20	0.00	5.00	166413428	25.00	5.00	95
100	0.00	82817975	0.20	0.00	5.00	414089868	25.00	5.00	100

Compound Interest Factors

Interest Rate, i	$(1+i)^{-n}$	$(1+i)^{n}$	$\left[\frac{i(1+i)^n}{(1+i)^n-1}\right]$	$\left[\frac{i}{(1+i)^n-1}\right]$	$\left[\frac{(1+i)^n-1}{i(1+i)^n}\right]$	$\left[\frac{(1+i)^n-1}{i}\right]$	$\left[\frac{(1+i)^n-in-1}{i^2(1+i)^n}\right]$	$\left[\frac{(1+i)^n-in-1}{i(1+i)^n-i}\right]$	
25.00%	Find P	Find F	Find A	Find A	Find P	Find F	Find P	Find A	25.00%
	Know F	Know P	Know P	Know F	Know A	Know A	Know G	Know G	
n	P/F	F/P	A/P	A/F	P/A	F/A	P/G	A/G	n
1	0.8000	1.2500	1.2500	1.0000	0.8000	1.0000	0.0000	0.0000	1
2	0.6400	1.5625	0.6944	0.4444	1.4400	2.2500	0.6400	0.4444	2
3	0.5120	1.9531	0.5123	0.2623	1.9520	3.8125	1.6640	0.8525	3
4	0.4096	2.4414	0.4234	0.1734	2.3616	5.7656	2.8928	1.2249	4
5	0.3277	3.0518	0.3718	0.1218	2.6893	8.2070	4.2035	1.5631	5
6	0.2621	3.8147	0.3388	0.0888	2.9514	11.2588	5.5142	1.8683	6
7	0.2097	4.7684	0.3163	0.0663	3.1611	15.0735	6.7725	2.1424	7
8	0.1678	5.9605	0.3004	0.0504	3.3289	19.8419	7.9469	2.3872	8
9	0.1342	7.4506	0.2888	0.0388	3.4631	25.8023	9.0207	2.6048	9
10	0.1074	9.3132	0.2801	0.0301	3.5705	33.2529	9.9870	2.7971	10
11	0.0859	11.6415	0.2735	0.0235	3.6564	42.5661	10.8460	2.9663	11
12	0.0687	14.5519	0.2684	0.0184	3.7251	54.2077	11.6020	3.1145	12
13	0.0550	18.1899	0.2645	0.0145	3.7801	68.7596	12.2617	3.2437	13
14	0.0440	22.7374	0.2615	0.0115	3.8241	86.9495	12.8334	3.3559	14
15	0.0352	28.4217	0.2591	0.0091	3.8593	109.6868	13.3260	3.4530	15
16	0.0281	35.5271	0.2572	0.0072	3.8874	138.1085	13.7482	3.5366	16
17	0.0225	44.4089	0.2558	0.0058	3.9099	173.6357	14.1085	3.6084	17
18	0.0180	55.5112	0.2546	0.0046	3.9279	218.0446	14.4147	3.6698	18
19	0.0144	69.3889	0.2537	0.0037	3.9424	273.5558	14.6741	3.7222	19
20	0.0115	86.7362	0.2529	0.0029	3.9539	342.9447	14.8932	3.7667	20
21	0.0092	108.4202	0.2523	0.0023	3.9631	429.6809	15.0777	3.8045	21
22	0.0074	135.5253	0.2519	0.0019	3.9705	538.1011	15.2326	3.8365	22
23	0.0059	169.4066	0.2515	0.0015	3.9764	673.6264	15.3625	3.8634	23
24	0.0047	211.7582	0.2512	0.0012	3.9811	843.0329	15.4711	3.8861	24
25	0.0038	264.6978	0.2509	0.0009	3.9849	1054.7912	15.5618	3.9052	25
26	0.0030	330.8722	0.2508	0.0008	3.9879	1319.4890	15.6373	3.9212	26
27	0.0024	413.5903	0.2506	0.0006	3.9903	1650.3612	15.7002	3.9346	27
28	0.0019	516.9879	0.2505	0.0005	3.9923	2063.9515	15.7524	3.9457	28
29	0.0015	646.2349	0.2504	0.0004	3.9938	2580.9394	15.7957	3.9551	29
30	0.0012	807.7936	0.2503	0.0003	3.9950	3227.1743	15.8316	3.9628	30
40	0.00	7523.2	0.25	0.00	4.00	30089	15.98	3.99	40
45	0.00	22958.9	0.25	0.00	4.00	91831	15.99	4.00	45
50	0.00	70064.9	0.25	0.00	4.00	280256	16.00	4.00	50
55	0.00	213821.2	0.25	0.00	4.00	855281	16.00	4.00	55
60	0.00	652530.4	0.25	0.00	4.00	2610118	16.00	4.00	60
65	0.00	1991364.9	0.25	0.00	4.00	7965456	16.00	4.00	65
70	0.00	6077163	0.25	0.00	4.00	24308649	16.00	4.00	70
75	0.00	18546031	0.25	0.00	4.00	74184119	16.00	4.00	75
80	0.00	56597994	0.25	0.00	4.00	226391973	16.00	4.00	80
85	0.00	172723371	0.25	0.00	4.00	690893480	16.00	4.00	85
90	0.00	527109897	0.25	0.00	4.00	#########	16.00	4.00	90
95	0.00	#########	0.25	0.00	4.00	#########	16.00	4.00	95
100	0.00	#########	0.25	0.00	4.00	#########	16.00	4.00	100

Introductory Structural Analysis Example Problems

A book of over fifty structural analysis example problems for engineers and engineering students taking courses in introductory structural analysis.

Example problems cover, equations of equilibrium, shear & moment diagrams, deflections and indeterminate structures using moment distribution. Two dimensional beams, frames and truss systems are used in the examples.

The Author has strived to present problems that would be found in a typical engineering class, in a hand drawn style that will be familiar to any student who has put pencil to engineering paper. (United States customary units)

Available on Amazon.com

Bridge Building Robots - ebooks for kids.

I have a bunch of ebooks about Bridge Building Robots for kids. A mix of adventure and bridges in every book.

Available on Amazon.com

Thanks for buying my Book!

"Never laugh at live dragons."

— J.R.R. Tolkien